CHARCOAL'S WORLD

CHARCOAL'S WORLD

Hugh A Dempsey

Western Producer Prairie Books
Saskatoon, Saskatchewan

Cover and book design by Warren Clark

Printed and bound in Canada by MODERN PRESS

1

Saskatoon, Saskatchewan

Western Producer Prairie Books publications are
produced and manufactured in the middle of
western Canada by a unique publishing venture
owned by a group of prairie farmers who are
members of Saskatchewan Wheat Pool. Our first
book in 1954 was a reprint of a serial originally
carried in *The Western Producer*, a weekly
newspaper serving western Canadian farmers
since 1923. We continue the tradition of
providing enjoyable and informative reading for
all Canadians.

Canadian Cataloguing in Publication Data
    Dempsey, Hugh A., 1929-
        Charcoal's world
        Bibliography: p.
        Includes index.
        ISBN 0-88833-003-0
        1. Charcoal (Kainah Indian) 1856-1896.
    2. Kainah Indians — Biography. 3. Indians
    of North America — Alberta — Biography.
    I. Title.
    E99.K15D44   971.23'00497   C78-002159-2

Contents

Preface

During the 1930s, a few Blood Indian children at Saint Paul's Indian Residential School were playing their favorite game. Two or three, who were the "bears," faced the wall at one end of the playroom while the rest, the "Indians," left their benches and began inching forward. Then, without warning, their attackers turned and, raising their arms in front of them, growled like grizzlies.

"*Tsa-ko*! *Tsa-ko*!" the girls screamed as the "bears" dashed after them. Quickly the hunted ones raced across the floor to the safety of the benches as they tried to avoid the growling attackers. At last each of the "bears" captured an "Indian" and returned to her station.

As the children played, an old woman hobbled down the road outside the school, her body bent, a shawl over her shoulders, and a dark kerchief covering her hair. Standing beside the fence, she spoke to some of the young students in the school yard, gave them candy, and told them to be good, honest girls. When they grew up, she said, they should all treat their husbands with respect.

An older pupil snickered nearby, and when the woman had left, the girl giggled aloud. "Look who's talkin' about bein' faithful to her husband," she laughed.

"Who is she?"

"Don't you know? That's Pretty Wolverine Woman. Long ago she was married to Charcoal — the same *Tsa-ko* you're using in your game. He's the boogey man of the Blood Reserve, and it's all because of his wife."

Over the years, Charcoal has become almost a legend among the Indians of southern Alberta. On one hand he is presented as some kind of terrible monster who frightens children when they misbehave. On the other, he is a hero with what seem to be supernatural powers.

A few of the elders still know the stories of Charcoal's exploits during the fateful autumn of 1896. In many ways, their stories agree with official reports of the Mounted Police, but the two sources diverge widely when they discuss the reasons for Charcoal's success and the cause of his eventual downfall.

Bits and pieces of the Charcoal story have been told to me during the past twenty-five years in idle conversations and in tale-swapping sessions. Some of the best information came from Charcoal's nephew, Big Sorrel Horse, while others who proved extremely helpful were George Calling Last, who had married Charcoal's daughter; Jack Low Horn; Jim White Bull; Laurie Plume; John and Albert Yellow Horn; Willie Scraping White; and a longtime historian of the Blood tribe, Mike Mountain Horse. These sources, coupled with the valuable court testimony contained in the Horace Harvey Papers (MG-30) in the Public Archives of Canada, have provided a valuable insight into the Indian side of the Charcoal affair. For too many years, people have accepted as final truth the cold, simplistic statements contained in the official reports of the North West Mounted Police and the Department of Indian Affairs.

Like so many situations involving Indian-white relations, there were two sides to the story, but only one was ever told. In many ways, Charcoal's one-man war against the white man is a classic example of Indian-white confrontation. It wasn't a case of the good guys against the bad guys, but rather of a clash between two cultures, neither completely understanding what was motivating the other. And like so many other frontier tragedies, a better understanding could have prevented it.

Appreciation is extended to the Blood tribe and friends on the Peigan Reserve who have assisted and counseled me. Many of them have passed away, but at this writing, Laurie Plume and John Yellow Horn stand in my mind as two men who are doing much to preserve the heritage of their respective tribes. My appreciation also goes to my wife, Pauline, who has translated some of the difficult Blackfoot words for me and has told me of her own Charcoal experiences while growing up on the Blood Reserve. And, as always, I must pay tribute to my late father-in-law, Senator James Gladstone, who was for many years my interpreter, friend, and counselor. Thanks also go to Jim Shot Both Sides, head chief of the Blood tribe, and to his council, to whom this manuscript was submitted for approval.

When an account such as this is based to a large extent upon oral history, it can include excerpts from actual conversations without slipping into the realm of fiction. When the old ones tell a story, it is presented just as if they had been there. Over the years, comparative studies have indicated that verbatim reports of conversations have been passed from one generation to the next with a high degree of accuracy, and so they are presented here in the form they were given to me.

Finally, thanks also are extended to those institutions which have aided me in my research. These include my own organization, the Glenbow-Alberta Institute, as well as the Oblate Collection in the Provincial Archives of Alberta, the Walter McClintock Papers in Yale University, and the valuable R.C.M.P. Papers in the Public Archives of Canada.

Chapter one

Charcoal was camped on the slope, looking out over the land. To the west the rugged line of the Rocky Mountains was silhouetted against the gray November sky. Southward, stretching before him, the rippling prairies undulated like snow-clad waves dashing against the massive base of Chief Mountain, that distinctive peak which projected from the mountain chain to form a landmark between the United States and Canada. Eastward from his vantage point, the rolling hills broke from their rhythmic pattern to become a flat and barren plain.

Bounded by mountains, hills, and distance, the land within his gaze looked like a separate corner of the world. And in a way it was. It was Charcoal's world, a place where he was born and a place where he soon would die. Down below, armed with guns, were men looking for him, to shoot him or to put a rope around his neck.

The Indian was armed with a .44-caliber Winchester, which he cradled in his arms. This gun, after all the days of running, hiding and starving, was now his only protector. His children had deserted him, his wives had flown, his brothers were in jail, and he believed that even his sacred powers could no longer help him. He was alone on the frozen slopes of the Porcupine Hills, alone with his horses and his gun.

A clump of trees in his camp had been drawn together by their crowns, to make a shelter where he could lie in relative comfort and security. A traveler might pass within a few yards of it and never know Charcoal was there. His scanty supplies reflected his desperate situation — a saddle pad, blanket, spy glasses, the clothes he wore, his rifle, and a broad knife thrust into his cartridge belt.

Charcoal knew he was going to die. At one time he might have asked his spirit protectors to keep him from that awful fate, at least until he had finished what he had set out to do. But it was not to be. He had abandoned his life by killing a man. The white man's law and the white man's holy book said that he had to die, so he had thrown his life away. He was like a warrior from those wild free days who rode ahead of the others into battle, wanting to die, knowing that he would be killed by enemy arrows. Like them he would go to the spirit world, and that time would be soon.

So much had happened. Forty winters earlier, in the year 1856, he had been born in the tepee of his father, Red Plume, a wealthy and respected warrior. The season had been a bad one, for in the late autumn the snows had swept across the prairies from the north, leaving deep drifts along the Bow and Oldman rivers. Then the warm chinook winds had come out from the mountains, turning the snow into slush until tiny rivulets ran in the coulee bottoms. After that, without warning, the cold Arctic winds had frozen the moisture into icy crusts which covered the land like a shiny blanket of crystal.

When the Bloods ventured from their lodges after the storm, they had found a vast sheet of ice. The horses had slipped and fallen, or torn their fetlocks when they broke through the jagged crusts. The hunters hadn't been able to chase buffalo, for the horses couldn't run; by the time spring came, many Bloods had died of starvation. It had been a winter of disaster, recorded by the holy men as *Itestsikakoy*, "the year we were slipping,"[1] and it was in that winter that Charcoal was born.

At the time the Bloods numbered 2,500 and were the second in size of the three tribes making up the Blackfoot nation. The largest was the Peigan, who ranged along the Missouri River in Montana, while the smallest was the Blackfoot tribe, who usually hunted along the Bow and Red Deer rivers. The Bloods, midway between their two neighbors, claimed the area of southern Alberta from the mountains to the Cypress Hills.

During Charcoal's baby years, there were no white men's forts in the Blackfoot hunting grounds, although the Indians had been trading with the British and Americans for almost 200 years. The closest posts were Fort Edmonton on the North Saskatchewan and Fort Benton on the Missouri.

As buffalo hunters, the Bloods had traveled in large bands over their broad domain. Leaders like Seen From Afar and Bull Back Fat could count on at least 600 warriors to protect the land. Incessant skirmishes with the Crow, Cree, Assiniboine, Kootenay, and Shoshone tribes became almost a game of war as horses were stolen, coups counted, and hunting parties driven away. Armed with flintlocks and bows, mounted on sturdy cayuses, and proud to the point of arrogance, the Bloods were living in their golden age.

As a child, Charcoal was named *Opee-o'wun*, or The Palate. This was just a baby name, one that would stay with him until he

2

earned his own name as a teenaged warrior. A name was a personal possession, something which was owned and used, like a knife or bow, then discarded when a better one could be gained. In this fashion, a man might go through life under four or five different names, giving one away as he took another. This was the way with Charcoal: as a boy he had been named The Palate, and later he had had the man's name of *Paka'panikapi*, or Lazy Young Man. This was no reflection upon his character; it was simply an old and honored name which existed in his family. Finally he took the name *Si'k-okskitsis*, or Black Wood Ashes, which the interpreters translated as Charcoal.[2]

Even as a boy, he hadn't been a big person, nor was he strongly built. Unlike some of his tribal relatives who were strapping six-foot warriors, Charcoal stood about five foot nine and was described as "thin, rather delicate looking, stooped, bow legged [and with] cheeks [that were] very much sunken."[3] When he was thirteen a terrible smallpox epidemic had struck him down, and although he survived, his face bore the deep pock marks of the dreadful disease.

The tribe had seen countless changes since Charcoal's birth. The white man's diseases of smallpox, measles, and tuberculosis had killed hundreds of the tribe. And when the buffalo were destroyed, the Bloods had to settle on their reserve or starve — or both. Bit by bit, their freedom had been whittled down until it had simply disappeared.

First had come their reliance on the traders for guns, knives, and kettles. Then there had been pressure to give up fighting, to live in peace, and to let the cursed Crees and mixed-bloods come into their lands whenever they pleased. Afterwards, with the buffalo gone, the white men had fenced them into reserves, keeping them alive — and quiet — with rations of beef and flour.

Charcoal was a member of a large family. His father, Red Plume, had two wives, the younger one, Killed Twice, being Charcoal's mother. The boy's only full brother was named Red Horse. His father's older wife, Longtime Buffalo Stone Woman, was a close relative of Seen From Afar, the famous warrior leader of the entire tribe. When he married, Red Plume decided to go with his wife to her more prosperous band, the Fish Eaters, and in the happy surroundings of that large camp, he too had become rich. From his older wife, Red Plume had five sons, Bear Back Bone, Left Hand, Knife, Running Crow, and Goose Chief, as well as two daughters, White Owl Woman and Weasel Foot Woman.

When he was young, Charcoal and his brothers may not have been the most popular men in camp, but they were recognized as warriors and leaders. Bear Back Bone was the oldest, but Left

3

Hand was the dominant one who ruled the family when their father became old and feeble. He was sometimes accused of bullying his friends, being disrespectful to his neighbors, and of being an uncertain ally in times of danger, but even if he was ornery and spoiled, he was still the leader of an important family. People could joke and gossip behind his back about the fighting that went on in his family, but no one would dare to be rude to him or his brothers.

Everyone remembered how Left Hand had become chief of the family group. The young men were resting quietly in camp one day when someone shouted that a Cree lying in ambush nearby had killed a Blood. Most of the chiefs were away hunting, so Left Hand had grabbed his gun and dashed to the hiding place, where he attacked and killed the Cree. As he rode proudly back to camp at the head of a party of warriors, he had proclaimed himself a chief. Even though the Fish Eater's camp was under the leadership of Red Crow, a man they all loved and respected, Left Hand's family from that time forward was recognized as a sub-band within the tribe.

It was customary for each band to have a distinctive name — Fish Eaters, Hairy Shirts, Lone Fighters — and before long Left Hand's followers acquired a title of their own. The Blood elders had made a peace treaty with the Crees, promising there would be no more war. But it was always the same; the old men made peace and the young ones made war. So it was with Left Hand, who attacked an unsuspecting Cree camp. As he galloped away triumphantly with captured horses, the angry Crees formed a revenge party and went after him. Left Hand managed to get back to the Bloods before he could be caught, but spoiling for a fight, he announced that he would lead a bigger party to attack the approaching enemy.

The elders were disturbed that the treaty had been violated, and as Left Hand tried to form his raiding party, the older chiefs stopped him. Angrily the warrior grabbed his gun and tried to leave, but the peaceful ones held him back. In frustration, Left Hand fired a shot into the air before stalking off to his tepee. The Bloods interpreted these actions as those of a spoiled, bad-tempered man who would not listen to wiser voices. And because of this incident, the sub-band had received its name; henceforth it was known as *Uspoki-omiks*, or Shooting Up. The title was no compliment, either to Left Hand or his relatives.

In spite of temporary restraint from the elders, the Shooting Up clan — including the teenaged Charcoal — had gone to war whenever the chance arose. It was customary for boys to have friends who were comrades, or *tukas*, on the warpath. Comrades looked after each other in times of danger and helped to share the

4

problems of the trail. And so it had been with Charcoal, whose companion was Always Takes the Gun, a boy his own age. Together they had gone on the warpath, both receiving honors for their successful horse raids against their enemies.

While Charcoal was still a teenager, the isolation of the Bloods from the white traders had suddenly ended when bearded men with barrels of whiskey came among his people. For many years, buffalo robes had been used by the traders for clothing, and there had always been a steady demand. But after the Americans found that the hides were good for industrial belting leather, they had wanted them by the thousands and been willing to pay high prices. Whiskey, repeating rifles, and other goods were bartered for the skins of the shaggy beast.

In no time the Bloods' hunting grounds were dotted with little log cabins where a buffalo robe would bring enough whiskey to keep a man drunk for two days. The Bloods no longer had to travel ten days to a trading post. Just as quickly as a hide could be cleaned and tanned, the whiskey was ready and waiting in exchange.

Before long most of the tribe had taken to drinking whiskey. Even the chiefs forgot their responsibilities as they joined in the rush to see who could get the most buffalo skins, who could be the most drunken — and who could live through the winter. In one season alone, the winter of 1872-73, whiskey claimed seventy lives among the Bloods. Some died of exposure while drunk, others were killed in brawls, and the rest succumbed to the poisonous effects of the brew itself. Under the guise of whiskey, the concoctions contained an assortment of ingredients to give them "bite and scratch" — red ink, bluestone, laudenum, chewing tobacco, soap, and red peppers. Even Red Crow was affected by the lethal brew and murdered his own brother in a drunken quarrel.

For a time it looked as though the whole tribe would destroy itself with liquor. Horses were traded for it, tepees became ragged and torn, people starved, and whiskey became the master of their lives. Perhaps that was why the red-coated policemen seemed to have magic powers. Where even the strongest warriors hadn't been able to keep the whiskey traders away, the North West Mounted Police who arrived in their land made the Americans disappear like dust devils. One week the bearded ones had been trading whiskey throughout the land; the next week they had vanished.

This happened in the autumn of 1874, when Charcoal was eighteen. The leader of the red coats, a man the Bloods named Bull's Head, met the chiefs and told them that his police were there to help the Bloods keep the whiskey traders away. And they had been true to their word: the traders stayed away and the Indians had begun to prosper. So these strangers who came from the rising sun were greeted by the Bloods as friends.

But their coming had bad effects too. Charcoal saw how the Bloods were stopped from going to war, how enemy camps of Crees and mixed-bloods came into their lands to hunt buffalo, and how the chiefs were powerless to stop them. With the arrival of the police, the Bloods ceased to be the masters of their own land.

A few years later, when the Indians were obliged to settle on a reserve, the last of their freedom was taken away from them. Since then, the Bloods as a tribe had been not unlike Charcoal was right now — marking time, waiting to die. With the buffalo had gone the happy nomadic ways; now they were mere anachronisms in a world controlled by the white man.

Chapter two

Queen Victoria was a very important person to the Bloods, even though no one from the tribe had ever met her. She was the one who had sent the police to make the treaty in 1877, and it was in her name that the red coats were now searching for Charcoal.

The first two decades under the Queen's law had been ones of privation and confinement. Like other Bloods, Charcoal had learned his bitter but imperfect lessons about the white man's law and knew what happened when the rules were broken.

In a way, it had all started in 1877 when messengers arrived to announce that the Queen wanted to make a treaty with them. The Bloods had no real desire to talk about treaties, so when the meeting place was set at Blackfoot Crossing, north of their hunting grounds, some of the chiefs had wanted to forget the whole proceedings. Finally Red Crow had decided they should go, and the tribe had arrived when the negotiations were almost over. So disinterested were the chiefs that many Bloods did not even bother to make the long journey. One of these was Charcoal, who was hunting far to the south with the Shooting Up band.

At the treaty negotiations, Crowfoot, the great chief of the Blackfoot, did most of the talking. Because of his influence with the Mounted Police, the four allied tribes of Bloods, Blackfoot, Peigans, and Sarcees chose him as their spokesman. When the discussions were completed, the tribes surrendered their vast hunting grounds to the Queen and agreed to take reserves at locations of their own choosing. But to most Bloods, the treaty was simply a promise from the Queen to look after them in case of starvation or epidemic and to give them five dollars a year in treaty money.

Although Charcoal missed the ceremony, he was on hand a year later when treaty payments were made at the Belly River, closer to home. For the first time, his name was entered into the government register; a Mounted Policeman inscribed "Charcoal" into the ledger, assigned him the number S-25, and paid him thirty dollars in treaty money for himself and his family.

By this time, Charcoal had taken his first wife, *Makaw*, and in 1878 their union had been blessed with a son. Yet when he came before the treaty table, Charcoal conveniently produced a family of a wife, a boy, and three girls, giving him a payment of six five-dollar bills.

In this apparent subterfuge Charcoal was not unique. Padding the annuity lists in order to gain larger payments was a common practice and one which later became the salvation of many families. To cheat the gullible white man was no crime; the Indians had lost their lands and their freedom to him, so they owed him neither gratitude nor trust.

Yet Charcoal's family did grow, for in the following year he took another wife, *Apinaki*, or Tomorrow Woman. However, he still managed to add at least two imaginary children to the paysheets, giving him an extra ten-dollar payment.

By 1879 the buffalo were virtually gone from Canada, so the Bloods followed the last herds into Montana. The Shooting Up band ranged far south to the Judith Basin, hunting what was left of the great herds. While there, early in 1880, Charcoal's first daughter was born to Tomorrow Woman. Named Owl Woman, she would be the only one of his children to reach maturity, dying at the age of twenty-six. Her older brothers were to die while still young, while another sister, baptized Bertha, born a few years later, would die at the turn of the century.

In the spring of 1881, Charcoal returned to Canada with the rest of the band, the last buffalo herds having been wiped out. As the Indians reached the Blood Reserve, they realized that their old way of life was gone and that they had no recourse but to turn to the Mounted Police for help. The once-independent warriors were now ragged and destitute mendicants who lined up each day for handouts of beef and flour.

Many people blamed the chain of disasters on the Blackfoot Treaty. After all, three leading chiefs had died within a year of its signing; even old Rainy Chief, the great Blood patriarch, had perished. Since then the land had been overrun by Crees and mixed-bloods, prairie fires had turned the land into a blackened wasteland, and now the buffalo had been destroyed. Where would it all end? Many Bloods believed the Indians would soon go the way of the buffalo, that they had become outcasts and aliens in their own land.

They knew the white man was at fault, yet instead of hating him, they resented and feared him. They did not understand those fair-skinned people who seemed to have the magical powers of *Napi*, the hero-trickster of Blackfoot mythology. And now the

8

white man's flour and cattle were all that stood between the Bloods and starvation.

In Canada, Charcoal joined Left Hand and his band on the Belly River, where they camped a short distance downstream from Standoff trading post. There he pitched his worn tepee near a backwater of the stream within view of the Waterton River. Sensitive and proud, he foresaw a bleak future which could be brightened only by the generosity of the white man. Resignedly, he accepted the new life and listened to the conciliatory words of his chiefs.

As soon as they were in camp, the Bloods settled into a monotonous routine. Those whose tepees were worn out were encouraged to cut cottonwood logs and put up crude shacks. Others, like Charcoal and his family, preferred to patch their old lodges and try to live as they had in the past.

But it was not the same. Three days a week Charcoal sent his wives to collect the beef and flour from the ration house. Because he had added to his family records, they got an extra pound each of beef and flour per day for every fictitious person on his ticket. The meat was often of poor quality and the flour was an unpalatable black, but at least there was enough to keep starvation away. Some of the more honest people, who had reported the true sizes of their families, were suffering and had to rely upon their neighbors for help.

Once in a while there was excitement in the camps when a few young men slipped away to raid the Crees in the Cypress Hills or when some whiskey was smuggled onto the reserve. But mostly the day's routine was a repetition of the previous one, as though they were marking time, waiting for the inevitable. First the buffalo had been taken away, then their freedom was gone, and soon the Indians themselves would disappear from the face of the earth. Each year dozens died from measles, influenza, or scrofula, but only a few babies were born.

In 1881, the daily ration was reduced to a pound of beef and half a pound of flour, and by 1883 the government agent had discovered the true size of Charcoal's family. Instead of receiving rations for eight people, as he had for two years, his ticket was now reduced to five. In a matter of months, his allowance of food had been drastically cut from eight pounds each of beef and flour to only five pounds of beef and two and a half of flour.

The Bloods were meat eaters who could consume huge amounts at a single sitting. A pot was usually boiling at all times, and members of the family helped themselves whenever they were hungry. Now, the reduced rations of beef, which often included large chunks of bone, were brought into Charcoal's lodge and were gone before the next ration day. To add to his problems

Charcoal's brothers were notorious beggars, and there was no way he could turn them away from his lodge when they wanted a meal.

After suffering through the winter of 1882-83, a desperate Charcoal sought his old companion of the warpath, Always Takes the Gun. Late in February 1883 they and a young boy named Red Paint plotted to kill a steer belonging to one of the nearby ranchers. They decided to travel downstream several miles to the Bell and Patterson lease, so that suspicion would not be directed to the Shooting Up camp.

But this was not to be.

The Mounted Police promptly noticed the suspicious tracks of unshod ponies heading away from the reserve and, following them, came upon the trio while they were still skinning the cow. Rapidly the police descended upon the culprits, arresting Always Takes the Gun and Red Paint before they could get away.

The resourceful family man, Charcoal, was not immediately caught. Mounting his horse, he galloped away as the patrol secured their other prisoners. When the two Bloods were brought to Macleod, the police learned that Charcoal had been the organizer of the raid and that he had shot the cow. A check of the reserve determined that he had fled, with rumors placing him a hundred miles north on the Blackfoot Reserve.

When Staff-Sergeant Horner was ordered to follow the fugitive, he left Macleod during a March snowstorm. Not expecting to be pursued in such bad weather, Charcoal rested comfortably with friends among the Blackfoot, and there he was easily apprehended. By 4 April he was in the Macleod guardhouse and committed for trial.

The young boy, Red Paint, was released with a warning, but Charcoal and Always Takes the Gun languished in jail for three months before appearing in front of Colonel Macleod.

A rash of cattle killings had occurred since the rations had been reduced, and ranchers were disturbed and angry. The local newspaper, *The Macleod Gazette*, demanded that action be taken and described Charcoal's crime as "one of the most deliberately planned and maliciously executed cases of cattle killing yet brought up." The magistrate agreed, told the pair they were "bringing disgrace to their whole tribe," and on 5 July sentenced them to a year in the Macleod guardhouse.[1]

For a man who had never known the confines of even a log house, the year in jail must have been a nightmare. A ball and chain were fastened to Charcoal's leg, and each day he was led out to exercise or to work within the walls of the fort. Night and day the Mounted Police were the masters of his life; whether he slept, ate, or worked, the police were there.

He would not have been comforted by the knowledge that his wives and children were alone with his relatives. Besides, their food supply had been further reduced, for while he was in jail his share of rations was suspended.

A month after he was sentenced, four of Charcoal's fellow inmates made a frantic bid to escape. With the help of another Blood, they freed themselves of their balls and chains while out exercising. The four men — two Stonies, a Blood, and a Peigan — dashed past the sentry and down to the underbrush near the river. The guard fired a number of shots, but the prisoners were soon out of sight. A short distance away, the Stonies separated from the other pair but were caught by an ex-policeman. A search party went in pursuit of the others, but they had escaped.

After that, life in jail settled into a dull and frustrating routine. The food was terrible. Stringy beef and bread was their unvarying diet, and considering that the police themselves protested the quality of the beef which was issued to them, the prisoners' food must have been leathery and almost inedible. The year must have seemed like a life-time to Charcoal who had known only the freedom of the prairies. To be confined to a reserve was humiliating enough but to be locked in an iron cage for trying to feed one's family was almost more than a man could bear. When he finally left the guardhouse in the spring of 1884, he carried with him deep and painful memories of prison and of the police who had pursued him and put him there.

At home Charcoal found that a number of changes had taken place. More Bloods were living in log cabins while several younger men and chiefs had turned to gardening as a form of livelihood. Neat rows of turnips, potatoes, and grain covered the river bottom in patchwork fields, while a few root houses were evidence that some harvests had been successful.

The year's separation had been bad for Charcoal's family, for *Makaw* had deserted him and although Tomorrow Woman remained, she had suffered near-starvation. The pair remained together for a few more months, but her health had so deteriorated that she died early in 1886. To fill his empty lodge — and bed — Charcoal promptly took another wife, Fisher Woman, by whom he had a daughter, Bertha.

The years on the reserve had not enhanced the popularity of Left Hand and his family. In fact, the sedentary life and the close confinement in the river valley had increased the gossip about the troublesome brothers and their family quarrels. On one occasion, when the Belly River changed its course and the backwater near the Waterton River dried up, everyone had laughed at the band's predicament. The backwater had been their source of water ever since they settled on the reserve, but now that it was gone they

11

were forced to move. Some people said the Shooting Up clan were so lazy they had loafed around all day gulping tea and had drunk the backwater dry. It was a big joke at the expense of the family.

Left Hand took his followers upstream several miles to Standoff springs where they pitched their camp a short distance from the Fish Eaters. Soon a small colony of cottonwood cabins arose in the timbered valley as the band settled permanently in its new location. But the Blood kept the joke about the backwater alive, so when another incident took place at the new location, everyone was jubilant.

Bear Back Bone had married a Sarcee woman and, like Charcoal's wives, she was subjected to the laziness of the spoiled brothers. Each morning when she arose, she went to the springs for water and soon had a large pot of tea boiling for her family. In the meantime, the other brothers arose one by one and seeing a fire in Bear Back Bone's place, they wandered over to share his tea. Once there, they settled down and stayed until the pot was empty.

After this had happened several times, Bear Back Bone's wife exploded in rage. "What kind of relatives do you have?" she demanded of her husband. "They do nothing but sit around all day and drink my tea!"[2]

When news of the argument spread, someone suggested that the name of the Shooting Up band be changed to the *Potstu'ki*, or Choking band. First they had drunk the backwater of the Belly River dry and choked off their fresh water, and now they were drinking the Sarcee woman's tea and choking off the supply for her family. The taunting name stuck, and from that time on, they were known derisively as the Choking band.

Charcoal was thirty-four years old in 1890 when Fisher Woman decided that she had had enough of the turbulent family. A daughter of Chief Sitting in the Middle, she returned to her parents' band with her daughter, leaving Charcoal with only his little girl, Owl Woman. But Charcoal did not stay alone for long. In the following year he married Pretty Wolverine Woman, or *Anu'tsis-tsis-aki*, a widow of twenty-six who had been married four times before, each time, to a man who was already married. She had simply become a second, third, or fourth wife. Her last husband had been Fox Head, who died in 1890, leaving her with two young boys, Bear Head and The Child. A forceful and strong-willed woman, she proved to be an ideal wife for Charcoal. She shared his intense interest in religion, as well as being an excellent mother and tireless worker.

During the next few years, Charcoal's daily routine was the aimless one of a young man forced to accept the fate which had befallen his people. In the mornings the horses were let out to graze, and sometimes he spent most of the day wandering with them. His wife got the firewood and water and cooked the food. With nothing to hunt, no enemies to fight, a man had little to do except look after his horses and join in the gambling or religious ceremonies which seemed to occur with increasing frequency.

Many Bloods found relief from their dull and oppressive life in the ritualistic mysticism of their own religion. The medicine bundles, ceremonies, secret societies, dances, and chants all were reminders of happier days, and when one thought about the past, he could sometimes forget the future. That was the way with Charcoal; he owned a Bear Knife, the soldier's medicine pipe, a painted tepee, and bundles which went with his memberships in the Horns and in the Dog Society.

In some ways, the Bloods were luckier than their Indian neighbors; their reserve was the biggest in Canada, and its isolation from larger towns and cities enabled the tribesmen to maintain many facets of their former existence. This made life more bearable, and it was possible to retain a certain amount of dignity. The wife could always be sent to collect the weekly rations, so that the warrior-husband would have no need to grovel before the Indian agent. Trips to town were made only when a man had money, perhaps from the treaty payments, so the traders treated him with respect. And within the tribe itself, people still recognized the feats of a warrior, the powers of a medicine-pipe holder, and the influence of a chief. If something occurred which was part of their new life, they usually followed the white man's rules, but for the rest of the time they tried to live according to their old values and practices. Sometimes it was hard, for often it was difficult to know just what the white man expected of them, but as long as they could remember the rules of the Indian agent, the police, and the missionaries, they could ignore the future and look only to each new sunrise.

But always the rules had to be remembered. Do not leave the reserve without a pass, or you will be put in jail. Do not steal the white man's cattle, even if he grazes them illegally on your reserve. Do not get caught buying whiskey from the bootlegger, or it will be seized. And never kill a man, or the police will put a rope around your neck and hang you.

These were the years when Charcoal was reduced to a shadow of a real Indian, for he acknowledged the superiority of the white man and, where necessary, set aside his own practices and beliefs. But beneath the docile exterior was the same kind of Indian who had once made the Blood tribe feared throughout the plains. During the years of oppression this side of him had been submerged, not destroyed. Only when the ultimate decision had to

13

be made — the fate of his own soul — did the proud warrior spirit emerge. It was there to help him die.

Chapter three

Charcoal was a proud man, and when he was told during the summer of 1896 that his wife was unfaithful, his first inclination was to throw her out of the house. She had already possessed four husbands before him, and somehow she drew men to her like moths to a flame. The couple had been married for five years, and he had treated her well, even paying for her leadership in the *Motokix*, the sacred women's society.

He learned about her infidelity just after he had followed the tribal custom of adding a second wife to his household. That spring he had married an attractive eighteen-year-old girl named Sleeping Woman, or *Iyokaki*, the daughter of war chief Medicine Calf. No one ever knew for sure if this marriage had anything to do with his wife taking a lover a few weeks later.

Charcoal was forty years old and Pretty Wolverine Woman was thirty-one. Living with them in their log house and tepee were Pretty Wolverine Woman's two children, Bear Head and The Child; Charcoal's sixteen-year old daughter, Owl Woman; and his new wife, Sleeping Woman. A short distance away was another tepee which was the home of Pretty Wolverine Woman's mother, Killed on Both Sides.

In September, word was received that the Cochrane Ranch wanted to hire a number of Indians to cut 400 tons of hay on its lease, some miles up the Belly River. Most of the able-bodied men in the Fish Eaters and in Charcoal's camp volunteered, and under the watchful eye of the Indian Department farm instructor, Cliff Clarke, they struck their tepees and moved off upriver. Among them were Charcoal, his two wives, and their assorted family.

Arriving at a large bend in the river, Charcoal and those in his band went a short distance west of the reserve to a small lake surrounded by low hills. Soon other tepees dotted the area as more and more Indians arrived. Some had their own mowers, and Clarke brought along government equipment for the others. By the time they were ready to start, seven mowers, four rakes, and thirty-three wagons had been assembled on the Cochrane lease. Under Clarke's instructions, hay was cut, loaded, and then piled in large stacks of 130 tons each. At the same time, extra hay was cut and delivered to the Indian hospital, the farm headquarters, and to the few Indians who operated their own ranches on the reserve.

Charcoal kept a suspicious eye on his erring wife, but his work in the hay fields was so demanding that he often was away for hours at a time. Sometimes Pretty Wolverine Woman accompanied him, but more often she stayed behind to carry out the chores around the camp. Soon the pressures of physical labor and worry about his wife began to undermine Charcoal's health. He had contracted tuberculosis, and sometimes he awoke in the morning with such sharp pains in his chest that he could not even drive his wagon to the field. Short-tempered, sullen, and bitter, he at last confronted his wife about his suspicions and forced her to reveal the name of her lover.

Her confession left him stunned and in a state of shock. Not only was the man six years younger than Pretty Wolverine Woman, but he was also her cousin. This put the entire affair on a completely different plane. Common ordinary infidelity might be countenanced and resolved, but a Blood Indian could never — never — have sexual intercourse with a direct relative. Not with a sister, an aunt, a cousin, nor anyone who shared a common ancestor. If this did happen, it brought shame to everyone, not just to the guilty pair, but to all who were close to them.

Charcoal was a member of the powerful Horn Society and the holder of medicine bundles and religious objects — all requiring honesty and fidelity from their owner. The Horn Society initiation ritual also involved his wife, who made profound commitments during the secret rites. But more important, Pretty Wolverine Woman was leader of the tribe's only society for women, the *Motokix*. Such a person was supposed to embody all that was pure and holy.

Instead, Pretty Wolverine Woman was having an affair with her cousin.

If the truth were known, Charcoal would be humiliated. A man who could not control his wife, who would permit her to commit such an outrage, could not be a guardian of the holy objects. Soon he could expect someone to come to him, pipe in hand, offering to smoke. While they shared the pipe, the man would announce his intention of taking over Charcoal's medicine-pipe bundle or his Horn Society bundle. Tradition would make it impossible for Charcoal to refuse, and soon he would be stripped of his bundles, disgraced, and everyone would know why —

16

because he couldn't control his wife and because he let her be penetrated by her cousin.

The young man who had debauched Pretty Wolverine Woman had a lengthy name, Medicine Pipe Man Returning with a Crane War Whoop, or *Nina'msko'taput-sikumi*. For the sake of brevity, the white man usually called him Medicine Pipe Stem. The full name referred to the owner of a medicine pipe who, many years earlier, had gone on a raiding expedition. As his party entered hostile territory, he had gone ahead to scout, and as he returned, he had given the cry of a crane to indicate he had found an enemy camp. Hence the name, which had subsequently been passed on from one generation to the next.

By 1896 this Blood libertine was twenty-five years old, lithe, handsome, and an acknowledged ladies' man. He had been in and out of several affairs, usually with married women, and had escaped with only minor rebukes. Even after he took Black Face's daughter as his mate, he had continued to lure other men's wives away for clandestine meetings in secluded coulees or in the dense brush along the river bottoms.

Medicine Pipe Stem was from a prominent family. His brother, Sleeps on Top, was one of the wealthiest men on the reserve, while his sister, Singing Before, was married to Red Crow, head chief of the tribe. Another brother, Yellow Creek, was a successful rancher.

Charcoal had known Medicine Pipe Stem all his life. Both lived along the banks of the Belly River, just upstream from the ration house at Standoff, and because Medicine Pipe Stem was so much younger, Charcoal usually called him *Saukomapi* — Boy. But the boy was now a man, and the dark clouds of disaster hovered over him.

At all costs, Charcoal wanted to keep the affair a secret. Otherwise it would destroy everything that was important to him. Instead of casting his wife aside, he swallowed his pride and angrily told her to summon her lover. When Medicine Pipe Stem entered their lodge he was disturbed to find both Charcoal and his wife sitting, grim-faced, waiting for him.

"Boy, listen to me," said Charcoal. "My wife is your relative. Stop your meetings with her at once, and tell no one about them. This will remain a secret among the three of us. I don't want anyone to know that I've discovered what's going on. People would have a very poor opinion of me if they knew. So end this now and I'll do nothing further."[1]

The meeting was over. No formalities, no shouting, no threats. Charcoal had delivered his message and he expected his advice to be followed. Medicine Pipe Stem, on the other hand, believed he had just spoken to one of the biggest cowards in the tribe — a man who was not prepared to fight for his family, nor even to demand a payment of horses for the dishonor which he had sustained.

During the next ten days, Charcoal continued to go out to the hay fields even when chest pains left him weak and nauseous. Part of the trouble, he knew, was from tuberculosis, the white man's disease which was eating away at his lungs. But the pain also came from the constant worry about his wife and her lover.

Finally, on 30 September Cliff Clarke announced that the hay contract had been filled and the work was finished. As they prepared to strike camp, Charcoal refused his wife's request that she go down to Standoff to collect the four days' rations for the family; he sent a young boy instead. Then, as the family was not to leave for the reserve until the following morning, he decided that a sweat bath might take away some of his tiredness and pain. Practiced both for reasons of religion and good health, the sweat bath had solaced him in the past, just as it had helped his people for centuries.

There was no wood near their prairie lake, so Charcoal instructed Pretty Wolverine Woman to catch her horse, hitch up her travois, and go to the river where she could find green willows for a sweat lodge frame and dry wood for the fire.

On the hillside overlooking Charcoal's camp, Medicine Pipe Stem sat beside his tepee, combing his long black hair. Always a vain man, he was proud of his good looks and often spent hours fixing his hair, cleaning himself, and gazing at his handsome face in a tiny mirror.

Just that morning he had broken his long silence and told his brother Yellow Creek all about his affair with Pretty Wolverine Woman. "Now go down and look at those lodges in the hollow," he said, "and see if you see anyone putting a travois on a pony."[2]

Dutifully Yellow Creek examined the scene at Charcoal's camp but saw nothing. A few minutes later, Medicine Pipe Stem leisurely strolled over to the edge of the hill and smiled. "There she goes," he laughed as he saw Pretty Wolverine Woman leaving the camp.[3] The woman looked up and, seeing her lover, made signs to him. He hurriedly checked his hair and, donning a new pair of moccasins, picked up his bridle lines and a horse blanket, and disappeared down the hill.

Charcoal had seen everything. Suspicious, he had squinted through the hole above his tepee door, observed his wife riding away, seen her making the signs, and then watched Medicine Pipe Stem going for his horse.

The younger man had expected Pretty Wolverine Woman to follow the trail to the Upper Agency, for he knew it was ration day and thought that she would, as usual, have plenty of time to make

18

the trip and to dally with him in some secluded grove of trees along the way. But he soon discovered his mistake, for he saw how the travois track left the trail and veered off towards the river, crossing to the other side. Pretty Wolverine Woman was already wandering about, collecting firewood, when her lover rode up and laughingly accused her of stealing his brother's firewood. By this time she was close to a corral and shed which belonged to Sleeps on Top. Pretty Wolverine Woman returned his good-natured joke, and soon they were both laughing as he dismounted and drew her close to him.

Meanwhile, Charcoal had caught his horse, picked up his rifle, and followed his wife. As he made his way through the brush, he heard the sounds of laughter. In the clearing, the whole un-believable scene unfolded before him — the travois and horse, another horse tethered to the same tree, and Medicine Pipe Stem standing with his arm around his wife's waist.

The angry husband dismounted and stalked across the pasture, ordering the man to let his wife go, but Medicine Pipe Stem merely stepped forward and mocked him. In his opinion Charcoal was a coward who would do nothing more than to issue meaningless warnings, just as he had done two weeks earlier.

"I'm not holding your wife," he laughed. "What's the use of getting angry? You're a very jealous man!"[4]

Then, as Charcoal raised his gun, the Indian laughed again. "What's the reason you're carrying your gun with you?" he asked, then coldly added, "I'll kill you first. I'm not afraid of you."

"You'd better not talk like that," Charcoal replied. "Only three of us know about this."[5] Then he pleaded with Medicine Pipe Stem to leave his wife alone. Four times he asked, each time a little more desperately than the last. Four times. Four was the most sacred number of the tribe. Chants were sung four times, rituals were performed four times, war exploits recounted four times.

Again Medicine Pipe stem responded with taunts. In those few moments of ridicule, Charcoal's world suddenly exploded. All the years of reservation life disappeared as if by magic. All the white man's rules were forgotten. It was now time to be a real Indian again, just as his father had been an Indian, and his father's father before that.

He, Charcoal, was the owner of the holy Bear Knife. When it had been hurled at him in ceremony and he had grasped it in the palms of his hands, he had received all the terrible strength of the grizzly bear. This was the animal which was most like man, yet it was wild, untamed, and free. The owner of a Bear Knife was not a meek coward to be mocked by a fornicating stripling. He was a man. A real man.

"I am going mad!" Charcoal screamed, and with tears running down his face, he turned and dashed into the brush.[6]

Both Medicine Pipe Stem and the woman misunderstood. Seeing his tears and hearing him shout in anguish, they were more certain than ever of Charcoal's cowardice. Even now, he was probably cowering somewhere in the trees, crying like a baby. Grasping Pretty Wolverine Woman by the waist, Medicine Pipe Stem led her into the cool darkness of the shed.

The man who stepped quietly from the brush a few minutes later was a different Charcoal. Calm, clear-eyed, and with strange coolness he crossed the pasture to the wall of the shed. Gaping holes between the logs where the chinking had fallen away exposed the couple to his view.

His wife was spread-eagled on her back, her cotton skirt pulled up well above her waist and her white blanket bunched on the earthern floor. Hunched over her, the straps of his overalls off his shoulders and the buttons of his trousers open in front, Medicine Pipe Stem was already in the act of intercourse. As they groaned and pushed and pulsated, neither heard the cartridge click into the chamber of the Winchester. Only when the barrel scraped between the logs did the gasping man look up. His last sight on earth was a flash of light as a bullet tore into his skull.

He was dead in an instant, his entire weight flopping heavily upon the panic-stricken woman. With his penis still within her, she struggled to free herself, shoving the body aside and scattering the beads from his necklace on the ground. At last she broke away from this embrace of death, gazing in terror at the sight before her. Then kneeling down, not sure that he was dead, she gently raised his head and placed his folded coat beneath it to comfort him. When she took her hands away, they were covered with blood and she knew he was gone. Tenderly she closed his eyelids and tucked his penis inside the overalls, accidently smearing it with his own blood in the process. The blue serge trousers that he wore underneath she left open, but the overalls themselves were carefully buttoned so that he looked almost like a man asleep. Only the blood which now soaked his shirt revealed the truth.

Charcoal had acted neither in anger nor in haste. The bullet had been perfectly placed right through Medicine Pipe Stem's eyeball without breaking the skin on either side. After his eyelids were closed, there wasn't a mark on his body, except for the blood which flowed from his nose and mouth. No marksman could have been more precise.

When Charcoal came into the shed, his gun hanging loosely at his side, his wife was cradling the body of her dead lover. Firmly, he pulled her to her feet but she turned on him savagely. "You want to get into trouble so bad," she spat, "you might just as well kill me too."

When he didn't answer, she begged him, "Kill me now," but he shook his head.

"No," he said quietly, "I'm not going to kill you. We'll wait until the police find out, and then we'll die together."[7]

Without apparent anger or concern, he led his wife over to the river, helped her wash the blood from her blanket, and returned with her to camp. Next morning they moved back to their log house on Bullhorn Coulee.

Chapter four

Samuel Benfield Steele, commanding officer of the North West Mounted Police, was posted twenty miles north of the Blood Reserve, just outside the windswept village of Macleod. His quarters looked out over the parade square where there was the constant activity of men coming and going. The two ancient cannon and the neat piles of iron balls had been swept clean by the yardbirds, and across the way, the men's quarters blended in with the bleak countryside.

Big and blustery, with a full mustache, Steele looked the part he played — the type of British officer who brought civilization to all the wildernesses of the world and taught the ruddy natives to obey British justice.

Sam Steele was a policeman's policeman. Intelligent, efficient, and active, he knew the Mounted Police handbook backwards and forwards, and was ready to toss it out the window if it didn't work. To him there were two kinds of law, the Queen's law and Steele's law, and both were right.

Seven years older than Charcoal, Steele had been born in Simcoe County, Upper Canada, of a British military family. He was a man from a different world than Charcoal's or, perhaps, from a different point in time. When Charcoal had been learning how to hunt birds with blunt-ended arrows, Steele was being tutored by an old English gentleman. When Charcoal was suffering through the agonies of smallpox, Steele was training to be a soldier in the Canadian militia. And as the blossom of Blood independence faded with the disappearance of the buffalo, the Mounted Police had become lords and masters of the great Canadian plains.

Sam Steele was one of the "originals" of the North West Mounted Police, having enlisted in 1873. He had taken part in the epic march across the plains, finally reaching Fort Edmonton at the end of the long journey. After distinguishing himself as a noncommissioned officer, he had risen through the ranks to become superintendent. Where Indians were concerned, he was sympathetic and straightforward. His goals were clear. They must obey the law, not question it; they must become civilized Christian people, not remain wild pagans; and they must give up detestable practices, such as native religious ceremonies, which had no place in the new order.

And if the Queen's law couldn't accomplish his goals, then Steele's law must. In 1884, for example, fears were expressed about the arrival of Louis Riel in the Saskatchewan country. Riel, the leader of the 1869 rebellion that had brought about the formation of the province of Manitoba, had since been an outcast and exile, living quietly as a school teacher in Montana. When he returned to Canada to take up the cause of his mixed-blood followers, messengers were sent out to spread the news.

One of these men, Bear's Head, was on his way to the Blackfoot Reserve when Steele's men intercepted him and sent him to jail for a month on a seldom-used vagrancy charge. At the end of that time he was ordered to leave the district. Instead, Bear's Head continued on to the Blackfoot camps where his presence was reported to the police. Surprised that the courier was still in the area, Steele sent a sergeant to arrest him, but the mixed-blood escaped custody by jumping from a slow-moving train.

Steele then took the matter personally in hand. With two constables he picked up Bear's Head's trail and followed it back to the Blackfoot Reserve. There he found the man in the lodge of the famous leader Crowfoot and demanded he be turned over at once. In an ugly confrontation with the Blackfoot chief, Steele had placed a hand on the butt of his revolver and hauled the mixed-blood outside.

"I told Crowfoot to come out of the tent so that I could speak to him," Steele later reported, "and that I had to have the half-breed dead or alive . . . that he, Crowfoot, had behaved badly, although he had always received fair play, that he acted as if he had been treated unjustly. . . ." Steele further insisted that Crowfoot come to the trial in Calgary. "You will find that you have been harboring a disturber of the peace," he told the chief.[1]

But this time Steele's justice didn't work. There were no charges outstanding against Bear's Head, and hence no reason for his arrest. The judge threw the case out and Bear's Head went free.

Almost the same thing happened in 1889 on the Blood Reserve. Six Indians had gone on a raiding expedition against the Crow Indians in Montana, but three were intercepted on the way back. After they had spent several weeks in the guardhouse, Steele

23

discovered that no one was coming from Montana to press charges, so the men were turned loose with a warning. The other three still at large were then invited into Macleod where Steele gave them a lecture on the evils of horse stealing.

Somewhere along the line communications broke down, and the Standoff detachment was never informed that the case was closed. On their books, the Bloods were still wanted for horse stealing. A few days later, when attending the Sun Dance, S. Sgt. Chris Hilliard and his men saw the "fugitives," but when they tried to arrest them, they were mobbed by angry Bloods who knew the real story.

When Steele learned that his men had been roughed up he sent a strong force out to arrest the culprits — in spite of the fact that Hilliard had tried to make an illegal arrest. Then, to compound the ludicrous situation and to underline Steele's attitude when dealing with Indians, the troublemakers were arrested without the benefit of warrants. With a sigh at seeing Steele's law once more at work, the judge dismissed the charges.

"In making this arrest, the non-commissioned officer was not in possession of a warrant," admitted Steele, "but I consider he acted perfectly right. There are so many bad Indians wanted at times that unless a man takes every chance offered he will likely lose his man altogether."[2]

Yet Steele was a good officer, one of the best in the force. He had the respect of his men and the support of the chiefs who wanted to co-operate with the new order. During Riel's second rebellion in 1885, Steele was gazetted a major and raised a troop of frontiersmen known as Steele's Scouts. They saw action against Big Bear's forces and succeeded in defeating them at Loon Lake.

During his years in the Mounted Police, Steele had seen the Bloods settle down to their new life on the reservation. He observed that log cabins had replaced tepees and that, by 1896, Chief Red Crow even owned a sewing machine and used table cloths. To Steele these were encouraging indications that the Bloods were becoming civilized and progressive. It seemed that he and the Indian agents were succeeding in their attempt to make the Bloods self-supporting.

This had been the dream of government officials as far back as 1880 when the Bloods first settled on their reserve. All the federal government needed to do, they said, was to give the Bloods rations for a few years until they had turned into farmers who could fend for themselves. Fourteen years later, the dream had not been forgotten, but its realization seemed far away. When it turned out that gardening didn't lead to self-sufficiency, the Bloods were urged to go in for ranching. They liked working with cattle and a few individuals became fairly prosperous, but self-sufficiency was still nothing more than an elusive dream.

In the meantime, native religion had been discouraged as Anglican, Catholic, and Methodist missionaries came to the reserve to open schools. At first, only the orphans or children of leading farmers went to classes, but enforcement of the compulsory-attendance regulations soon took many more away from their homes and into boarding schools.

Steele encouraged these changes, for he saw that the Bloods could not remain completely isolated from the developments taking place around them. Their vast reserve, some fifty miles long and thirty wide, was like an island in a sea of prairie grass, yet the waves of European civilization were lapping at its shores. To the south, Mormon settlers had built the town of Cardston and were irrigating scattered farms throughout the region. The land to the west was taken up by the huge Cochrane lease, while smaller leases bordered the northern and eastern parts of the reserve. Now the days of the big-time ranches were passing, and small farms were already beginning to encroach upon the cattle ranges.

To men like Steele, these were signs of progress, and if the Bloods were to survive, they would need to change with the times. Only four years earlier, the railway had reached their main marketing town of Macleod, just east of Major Steele's headquarters, providing a tangible link with the outside world, and their chiefs Red Crow and One Spot had even traveled to Toronto and Ottawa to see how the white man lived.

The Bloods' other marketing town, Lethbridge, had become a large coal-mining center where the Indians often seemed out of place among the polyglot confusion of Italian, Welsh, and Slavic miners.

Steele saw his role as that of a policeman who had to maintain the Queen's law but at the same time to extol the superiority of the British way of life. To keep the Bloods in line was part of his responsibility, but to discourage their outmoded practices and beliefs was also essential if they were ever to accept the white man's ways.

It was as simple as that.

Chapter five

The first hint of trouble for Major Steele came innocently enough. On 10 October Sleeps on Top and Yellow Creek stopped at the Indian agency to see if anyone had heard from Medicine Pipe Stem. Nobody had seen him for ten days, not since Yellow Creek had watched him leave the haying camp with his bridle lines and saddle blanket.

Although they wouldn't explain what was behind their suspicions, they thought he had been murdered, and they wanted the Mounted Police to start an investigation. When Agent James Wilson tried to press them for information, they became evasive but insisted the boy must be dead.

Just a few weeks earlier, Wilson had heard that Eagle Shoe was looking for the young rascal after some mix-up with his wife. And a while before that, Medicine Pipe Stem had given a local trader two dollars, with instructions to tell a certain married woman that it was hers to spend.

"Knowing the young man well," Wilson later wrote, "and having seen him a short time ago, and also knowing his reputation for being mixed up in women scrapes, I told these Indians I did not feel justified in calling out the Police for any such purpose, and asked them to go to his relations at the South Peigan Agency. There, I told them, I thought he must have gone with some woman."[1]

The brothers felt it was no use going there, but Agent Wilson wouldn't listen. If they wanted a search made, they would have to do it themselves. He would even give them a pass so they could search the Cochrane lease.

Next morning, Sleeps on Top, Yellow Creek, and Wolf Tail went back to the haying camp to see if they could trace the missing man's path. As they prowled through the brush, they passed close to the cowshed, but no one looked inside. One of the searchers found a set of bridle lines, which Yellow Creek identified as his

26

brother's, but a thorough examination of the area turned up no further clues.

During the afternoon, a rider galloped up with the news that Wolf Bull's daughter claimed to have seen a dead body. That evening, Sleeps on Top rode over to the neighboring camp where the daughter, Trouble Shining, told her story.

"I went with the other women to get wood. Rag Woman, Fishing Woman, Hairy Woman, Pipe Woman and Singing on the Shore were with me. I was on the fence when I first saw him. He looked like a dead man. I was going to go into the house, but Rag Woman told me not to, and she stopped me."[2] She went on to describe the building, which Sleeps on Top recognized immediately as his cowshed.

It was too late to ride the twenty miles back upriver, but next morning the search party set out, and by afternoon they were gazing silently upon the body of the dead lover. Medicine Pipe Stem lay stretched out on his stomach, his head resting on his folded coat. Gently, they rolled him onto his side, observing the dried blood crusted on his shoulder and a dark stain discoloring the ground.

They could see he had been dead for several days, but there wasn't a wound on his body. As the women wailed the terrible banshee cry of the dead, the men stood silently for a few moments, tears running down their cheeks. One of them began talking in a low voice, telling Medicine Pipe Stem how they would miss him, how his handsome smiling face would never again be among them, and how they would never again hear him speak or laugh.

Later that evening, the distraught brother arrived at the Lower Agency, where he gave the news to Agent Wilson. It was too late to confirm the report that night, but the agent notified Major Steele in Fort Macleod and asked him to send out the coroner. The Mounted Policeman reacted routinely and without concern — it could be a case of suicide, alcohol poisoning, almost anything at all. Word was sent to the local watchmaker, W. S. Anderton, who doubled as coroner when the need arose, and a scout was dispatched to the Big Bend outpost with instructions to Insp. A. M. Jarvis to investigate.

Besides the high rate of mortality from measles, tuberculosis, and assorted diseases which infected the reserve, Steele had investigated a number of other deaths there. One occurred when a woman ate the stale beans given to her at the Standoff outpost. A man had died when his wagon overturned on him. And just a month earlier, Little Bear had drowned in the river while washing his hair.

But just to be on the safe side, Steele sent along the police surgeon, Dr. C. S. Haultain, in case the coroner needed help. After all, there was blood but apparently no wound.

That same night, Charcoal also heard about the discovery of the body. For the past few days stories had been circulating about Medicine Pipe Stem's disappearance. Some shared the view that he might have been killed, but if that were the case, suspicion centered upon Eagle Shoe who had openly threatened to beat the young man if he ever caught up with him.

On Monday evening, 12 October, when Sleeps on Top passed through the Upper Agency on his way to Wilson's house, he spread the word about his brother's death. For twelve days, Charcoal had waited patiently for the news. Now it had come. He was no longer a part of the real world around him but was a man between two worlds, waiting for death.

When Charcoal killed Medicine Pipe Stem, he had been following the ways of the old ones. He believed the Bear Knife had given him the strength to kill his enemy, just as it had always helped warriors in battle but after he had committed the deed, he realized that his life was finished, for he had broken the white man's most important rule; never kill, or the police with put a rope around your neck.

Charcoal never fully understood the ways of the white man. No one explained to him such terms as "manslaughter," or "justifiable homicide," or "extenuating circumstances." He had no way of knowing that if he surrendered and confessed there probably would have been a brief court trial and he might even have been released. All he knew were the simple facts which the Mounted Police and missionaries had been pounding into his head for a quarter of a century. Do not kill. Thou shalt not kill. Never kill. Murderers are hanged. To kill is to murder, and to murder is to hang.

So on that fateful day, the bullet that had killed Medicine Pipe Stem had also meant the death of Charcoal. It was as simple as that. Charcoal, in that instant, had chosen to follow an ancient tradition of his tribe — *iskohtoi-im'ohk'si-ow*. He had decided to "sacrifice himself" or "throw his life away." He had thereby become a dangerous man, not only to his enemies, but to everyone around him. It was all part of the old way of life, the Indian way.

In the old days, if a man knew he was going to die of some illness or infirmity, he would go to war with no intention of returning alive. Often he did not even let his comrades know his plans, but once they were in hostile territory, he boldly set forth to find an enemy camp. Once there, he sang his war song, tauntingly screamed his war cry, and galloped forward into the rain of enemy bullets and arrows. Before he died, he tried to kill as many of the enemy as possible, heedless of his wounds and his certain death.[3]

Yet this warrior was not being foolhardy, for his only concern was his future life in the spirit world. If he chose to stay at home, lingering meekly unto death, he would creep into the land of the dead like a child or an old woman. But if he rode into a hostile camp and killed their young men, then everything would be different. The slain enemy would enter the land of the dead before him, and when the spirits asked who had killed them, they would speak his name. Then, when death finally came, he would ride into the shadow world with pride and dignity; the spirits would recognize his name and welcome him. In that ghostly land in the Sand Hills, he would arrive like a great leader, not like some stray dog.

In the 1870s, after the Mounted Police came, the days of fighting had ended. What could a warrior do now? There were no more enemies to kill, no more messengers to send to the spirit world to prepare the way for the dying man.

Or were there?

Gradually a new philosophy had grown upon the old. The messenger did not need to be an enemy; any important leader would do. He, too, would go to the land of the dead and speak the name of his killer. The spirits would nod their ghostly heads and murmur to themselves that if this messenger was a respected leader, then the name he uttered must be that of a man even greater than he. Thus, the way would be prepared.

For Charcoal, the killing of a chief or white official — or both if possible — would ensure him a satisfactory entry into the spirit world. This was not merely a whim or an imitation of the white man's philosophy of "being hung for a sheep or a lamb." Rather, it was a real part of Charcoal's world, where the supernatural was never too far away from daily life.

Religion had always been important to Charcoal. Like others in the tribe, he was surrounded by spirits of good and evil which could affect his hunting, his horse breeding, or his family's health. One way to gain influence, both with the spirit world and with those in his tribe, was to join in the secret ceremonial life of the reserve.

Charcoal had done this willingly, for he shared the strong beliefs about the spiritual powers which went with native rituals. As a young man he had been initiated as one who could cut the rawhide ropes for the Sun Dance lodge. For this he had been painted and taught the songs of Morning Star, the mythological sky man who had sent the ceremony to earth. Then, as a warrior, Charcoal had taken the Soldier's Pipe, becoming one of the select group of medicine-pipe owners. These men had the power to cure

29

the sick and to pray for those in trouble. After the first thunderstorm each spring they gathered to open and renew their sacred bundles.

Charcoal owned a tepee which was painted with a mountain design. For this he had special songs, as well as the altar, bundle of sweetgrass, and sacred buffalo stones that went with it. He also possessed a weasel-tail shirt and ermine-fringed leggings, each of which had holy songs and supernatural powers. Then too, he was a member of the Dog Society, a religious body consisting of men of the same age, and of the Parted Hair Society, which performed special prairie-chicken dances learned from the Assiniboines.

But Charcoal's two most important commitments to his religion were his membership in the Horn Society and his ownership of a Bear Knife. The Horn Society was the most secret and the most revered organization on the reserve. Although its main purpose was to cure the sick and bring good fortune to the tribe, its powers were so strong that its participants were generally feared.

"The members of the Horn Society are regarded as very powerful men and women," a Blood woman once explained. "It is very dangerous even to talk about them and one must not tell what is done in the society; ill luck will surely befall him if he does. The ceremonies are secret. The power of members is so great that to wish anyone ill or dead is all that is needed to bring the realization."[4]

According to tribal lore, the society originated in the experiences of a man who married a spirit woman — a cow buffalo who had taken on human form. She bore him a son but warned him that he must never strike her with fire. One evening, however, he became angry with the way she had prepared food for his guests, so he struck her with a blazing stick from the campfire.

Immediately the woman and boy vanished. The distraught Indian went in search of them, finally discovering that they had been turned back into buffalo. When he came to their herd, the buffalo leader said if he could pick his son from the dancing calves four times, his family would be returned to him. Before he started to choose, his son whispered that he would hold his tail in the air as a sign.

The second time, the boy closed one eye and his father chose correctly. The third time he let one ear hang down, and for the fourth choice, he told his father he would hold up one leg. This time, however, another calf noticed his unusual dance step and decided to imitate him. The father guessed wrong, whereupon the herd trampled him to death.

Later, as the cow and calf mourned over his broken body an old buffalo bull took a piece of the Indian's bone into a sweat

30

lodge and restored the man to life. After this had been done, he turned the cow and calf into humans, teaching the man the ceremonies of the Horn Society and his wife the rituals of the sacred women's society.

When Charcoal decided to join the secret society, he and his wife were taken with other initiates to a special lodge made of travois, tepee poles, and canvas. There they spent the night being painted, exchanging clothes with old members, and receiving the bundles, spears, staffs, and crooks which constituted the Horn regalia. People spoke only in whispers about the actual transfer ritual itself, and of the strange rites performed by the members and their wives long after sunset.

Many of the ceremonies imitated the actions of the buffalo. In the nomadic days members had hoped that this would bring them a good hunt. By Charcoal's time, of course, the buffalo were only a memory, but each year the ceremony was performed, not for the return of the shaggy beast, but for the survival of the tribe.

Membership in the Horn Society was expensive, so only the most wealthy and dedicated ever joined. The fact that Charcoal was a member, besides being involved in several other religious societies, indicated the strength of his belief and the wealth of his family. On the other hand, his ownership of the Bear Knife was evidence of the strong warrior spirit which lay beneath the surface of the mild-mannered man. The Bear Knife, a double-bladed weapon with the jaw of a grizzly bear attached as a handle, symbolized the freedom which the Bloods had once prized.

The knife had originated through the experiences of a warrior named Berry Child. While still a youth, he had left his camp in search of a vision that would give him protection and power. Discovering the cave of a grizzly bear, he had remained there without food or water for four days, until the vision of a bear came to him in a dream. It ordered him to go to the land of the Underwater People where he must take from them the blade of a knife. From there he was told to travel to the middle of a swamp to find the skeleton of a huge bear. After fastening the jawbone to the blade, he had to climb a high mountain until he reached a meadow where a lodge had been pitched. There an old woman would decorate the knife with eagle feathers, make a scabbard of otter skin, and give him the power of the bear.

When Berry Child had fulfilled these tests, he returned to his people with the songs and rituals of the Bear Knife. The spirit also taught him how to transfer it to others; this was the ceremony used when the fearsome weapon was given to Charcoal. While seven men stood outside the tepee, the old owner sprang on Charcoal and threw him into a pile of rose bushes which had been piled near the back of the lodge. While the other men fired their rifles,

31

the owner painted Charcoal with a mixture of ocher and gunpowder, at the same time pressing the sharp thorns against his naked body.

As the ceremony continued, Charcoal was obliged to crawl upon the ground where he was struck several times with the flat side of the knife and hurled back into the thorns. At one stage, the owner savagely stabbed the knife into the earth, singing, "I am looking for someone to kill."

When Charcoal was being painted, he was taught a song he could sing while pursuing an enemy:

> I will run after him.
> He will fall.
> I will stab him.[5]

He was told that if an enemy shot at him, he was not to dodge but to attack. The blade was to be painted with a zigzag blue line to give it power and incense of parsnip root was to be made for it three times daily. At the end of the ritual, the Bear Knife was hurled at Charcoal in such a way that he had to catch it between the palms of his hands; if he missed, it could kill him.

Many stories were told about the power of the Bear Knife. On one occasion, White Calf and Chief Paint had gone to raid the Crow Indians, but they were discovered. When they reached a creek bed, Chief Paint had crawled into a cave to hide while his comrade, who owned a Bear Knife, remained outside to fight. As the Indian lay inside, he heard the sounds of battle, followed by the roar of a bear attacking the Crows. When Chief Paint came out, his friend told him that a bear had come to his rescue, but many believed that White Calf himself had turned into a grizzly.

Later, when he was camped on Blackleaf Creek, White Calf's camp had been raided by another Crow war party. White Calf had pulled off his moccasins and said to his wife, "Scratch my feet. I'm going to turn into a bear."[6] But she was afraid, so he fought in the form of a man.

By the 1890s, when the Bear Knife came to Charcoal, it had been handed down through several generations and had a solid reputation for savagery and supernatural power. This knife, as well as his membership in the Horn Society and possession of other religious objects, gave Charcoal the ability to pray for people and to bring them good fortune. In this way, he became an Indian doctor, treating the sick in the village. Even the great holy man Fire Steel brought his son to Charcoal to be cured.

With these supernatural forces guiding his life and his belief in the spirit world governing his death, Charcoal decided to follow the old ways. After killing Medicine Pipe Stem, he believed he must die, but he chose to go like a warrior in battle. Concerned about his need for a spirit messenger, he decided that he would slay the greatest leader on his reserve — Red Crow, the head chief of his tribe. When dead, the spirit of this leader would enter the ghost world before him. After that had been ensured, Charcoal could kill his unfaithful wife, commit suicide, and make his way to the shadow world.

As soon as he learned that Medicine Pipe Stem's body had been found, Charcoal knew it was time to act. He caught his bay horse and rode out into the darkness, his rifle resting easily across his saddle. Quietly he followed the trail upstream to the Fish Eaters' camp, veered off into the trees, and trotted up to Red Crow's stable.

There were only two people at home, the head chief and one of his wives, Charging Last. She saw the dark figure ride slowly towards the kitchen, and when she recognized Charcoal, a sudden fear gripped her. She had been told about the trouble at the hay camp and knew instinctively that Charcoal had decided to throw his life away.

"Don't come out," she whispered loudly to Red Crow. "There is something wrong with this man riding round the house."[7]

As the husband crouched by the window, Charcoal dismounted and began walking towards the building. He was within twenty feet of the door when one of the dogs which had been sleeping nearby suddenly became aware of the stranger. Jumping to its feet it began to bark and growl, soon to be joined by several others. Charcoal hesitated, then ran to his horse, and rode off into the darkness.

Back on the trail, the Indian reconsidered the situation. He could not get close enough to kill Red Crow, but he still needed his ghostly messenger. Then the thought struck him; he would kill the Indian agent, James Wilson, the man they called *Mo'kski*, or Red Face. He was their grandfather chief and would be a fit person to tell the spirits that Charcoal was coming. From the Fish Eaters' camp, Charcoal continued his journey up the Belly River, passing the Mounted Police detachment at Standoff on the other side of the stream. Keeping close to the river, he crossed several coulees below the towering cliffs of Belly Buttes, arriving at last at the Lower Agency.

Again his luck was bad. The agent's house was in darkness, and although he gazed into all the windows, he could see no one inside.

Turning westward towards home, Charcoal retraced his route past the buttes and the police detachment. Then, as he passed near the home of Edward McNeil, the farm instructor, he saw a light in his window. Without a moment's hesitation he turned into the lane near the yard where cattle were slaughtered for the Indians' rations and reached the house without going near the Indian cabins and their noisy dogs.

McNeil had just finished writing a number of reports and was gathering his papers together for next morning. He was expecting to have a busy day, starting with a trip to the sawmill, and continuing on to the Mormon settlement to buy cattle. As Charcoal peered through the window, his rifle cradled in his arms, he was ready for instant action. The window blind had been pulled, but a flowerpot on the sill prevented it from going all the way down. It left just enough room for Charcoal to see the farm instructor moving about inside.

Waiting patiently in the darkness, the Indian watched until McNeil was passing close to the window, his whole body silhouetted by the lamp on the table. Raising his rifle and aiming for the heart, Charcoal carefully squeezed the trigger.

Crash!

The exploding bullet and smashing glass echoed along the valley as McNeil spun around and fell to the floor. In an instant, Charcoal was gone, only the muffled hoofs marking his route into the quiet autumn night. He had done it! Now he had a messenger to the shadow world.

Chapter six

Next morning, 13 October, Sam Steele learned that Farm Instructor McNeil had been shot and wounded. He was not really surprised, for ever since some Indian troubles in the previous year, he had been expecting something to happen among the intractable Bloods. He remembered well the day he had opened a copy of *The Macleod Gazette* and seen the item from Prince Albert, over in the Saskatchewan country. A young Cree Indian named Almighty Voice had escaped from the guardhouse at Duck Lake, and when Sergeant Colebrook had tried to recapture him, the policeman had been shot and killed.

Something was going wrong.

The reserves had been quiet for the past few years, and it had looked to officials as though the Indians were at last on the road to becoming civilized. They were well behaved and seemed to have accepted their new way of life. Shirts and trousers were more common than leggings and blankets, and a few of the younger men were learning English. Quite a number of students were attending the day schools on the reserves while others were living in church-operated boarding schools. Gardens and cattle herds showed that many of the Indians were working hard to supplement their rations. In his outposts, Steele even employed Indian scouts to go on patrols and to help police.

Although there had been some minor incidents of petty theft, drunkenness, and internal squabbling, most of the reserves appeared to have become quiet, law-abiding communities. But in 1895, a few clouds of trouble had darkened the horizon. On two occasions, white men had been wantonly murdered by Indians. One of the victims had been a Mounted Policeman and the other an ex-member of the force.

The first murder had taken place on the neighboring Blackfoot reserve. According to newspaper reports, Francis Skynner, the ration issuer, had opened his door on the evening of 3 April, and someone had killed him. Skynner, an ex-corporal in the Mounted

Police, was said to have been a tactless, unpopular man who had not even bothered to learn Blackfoot. The articles attributed the killing to a man named Scraping Hide, whose nine-year-old son had just died. Apparently, when the boy was ill, the Indian had gone to Skynner, begging unsuccessfully for a little meat so that he could make some beef tea. On a second occasion, when Scraping Hide returned to the ration house to repeat his request, he again was refused, whereupon he swore that if the child died, the ration issuer would die too.

Another version of the story, probably the correct one, was that the boy had contracted tuberculosis while away at school and had died a day after being released. Scraping Hide had brooded about the death for a month, then decided to take his revenge on a white man before committing suicide. He first went to the home of the farm instructor, G. H. Wheatly, but finding him absent, he proceeded to Skynner's place where he had more success. When the police arrived on the scene, the issuer's body was sprawled near the door, his brains splattered all over the porch.

The Indian agent and Constable Rogers learned that the killer had fled to the Blackfoot cemetery where he was waiting on his son's grave for the police to attack. Standing within a few feet of the monument to Chief Crowfoot, he danced and waved his gun, threatening to shoot anyone who came near him. For two days he stayed by the grave, shooting at police and volunteers who tried to talk him into surrendering. At last, Constable Rogers returned the fire, driving the Indian down the hill and into a marsh where he shot and killed him.[1]

It seemed a tragic, senseless killing, but not so frustrating as the Almighty Voice affair. Late in October 1895, a young Cree from One Arrow's band, whose land adjoined the Saskatchewan River, had killed a cow for a wedding feast. Arrested by the Mounted Police on the following day, he had been placed in the guardroom of the Duck Lake detachment to await trial. In the night, while the guards were sleeping, he had slipped through an unlocked door, swum across the freezing river, and returned to his reserve.

For the next few days, the Mounted Police made periodic raids on the One Arrow Reserve, hoping to find Almighty Voice at home or with friends. Then word came that the young fugitive and his bride were on their way to the John Smith Reserve, some distance to the north. In hopes of intercepting the pair, Sgt. C. C. Colebrook and scout Francis Dumont followed the trail and found their camp a few miles south of the reserve.

As the Mounted Policeman rode forward, Almighty Voice called out in Cree, warning him to stay away or take the risk of being shot. When the message was interpreted, Colebrook decided to ignore the threat and draw his revolver. At that moment,

Almighty Voice raised his .45-.75 Winchester and shot the policeman in the chest.

After the police scout had fled, the young Cree took Colebrook's revolver and horse, and struck camp. By the time Dumont returned with help, the policeman was dead and the fugitive had disappeared.[2]

Major Steele saw the notice of the murder in the Macleod newspaper, but in the weeks that followed, there was nothing further to report. Although patrols scoured the area, Almighty Voice could not be located. Within a short time, it was evident that the Indians from the One Arrow Reserve were hiding the wanted man and in spite of threats, pleas, and finally a $500 reward, no trace of him could be found.

Steele had no way of knowing, of course, that Almighty Voice would outlive Charcoal, by remaining at large throughout 1896 and into the spring of the following year. Only after he was trapped in a grove of trees with his two cousins and bombarded with cannon shells was the elusive Indian finally, and utterly, destroyed. But before he died, Almighty Voice killed two more white men, one a policeman, and wounded another four.

At one point, when Almighty Voice and his cousins were surrounded, there was an opportunity for him to escape. Instead, the young fugitive chose to remain in the trap, waiting for the inevitable death, a warrior's death. This was something the white man would never really understand. It was not part of his law.

Perhaps it was only a coincidence, but soon after the troubles involving Scraping Hide and Almighty Voice, Charcoal's people reemerged from their months of passivity to challenge the authority of the Mounted Police. For the first time in many months, cattle began to disappear from the nearby Cochrane Ranch, and in November 1895, Major Steele and the Indian agent were obliged to set up a series of patrols which would take Indian scouts into the areas where the herds were grazing.

Two months later, the trap closed on Charcoal's twenty-year-old nephew Crane Chief and another Blood named The Glove, who were charged with cattle killing. When the case came up before the magistrate, the two men were proven to have had frozen beef in their possession just after one of the Cochrane's cows was slaughtered, but there was insufficient evidence to proceed with a trial.

Instead of being frightened by this near brush with prison, Crane Chief became more daring. Drawing a number of friends and relatives around him, he assumed leadership of a party of raiders that killed cattle from nearby ranches during the ensuing months.

The end finally came when one of the women in the party,

Running Everywhere, got into an argument with the other rustlers and rushed off to tell the police all she knew. Within a short time, Steele's men had arrested Charcoal's nephew, as well as three other men — Many Different Axes, Shouts in the Middle, and Wounded Before — and two women, Longtime Treaty Woman and Round Body Woman. This time there was direct evidence supplied by the willing informant so the entire group was thrown in jail to await trail later in the fall. Crane Chief's father, Bear Back Bone, made an appeal on behalf of his son but was told that the young warrior had been the leader of the gang and instigator of cattle killing.

This kind of trouble had been serious enough, but now Major Steele was faced with a situation potentially as dangerous as the Almighty Voice or Scraping Hide confrontations. On 12 October, someone had taken a shot at Farmer McNeil, and the bullet would likely have killed him had it not been deflected downwards by a plant in the window so that it entered the man's side just above the hipbone. Although knocked down by the blast, McNeil had been on his feet a few minutes later, helping to search for the culprit. Afterwards, he had walked over to the Catholic mission and was now resting comfortably in their hospital.

S. Sgt. Chris Hilliard of the Standoff detachment was investigating the incident, but there seemed to be no clues. McNeil could not name anyone who hated him enough to lay in ambush for him, but he promised to review his activities to see if he had done anything that might have caused an Indian to turn against him.

In the meantime, the coroner and his jury of local ranchers took a late afternoon ride upriver to the cowshed. The exact cause of Medicine Pipe Stem's death was still unknown, and the police had no evidence to connect Charcoal with either shooting. Nor was there any obvious link between the two cases.

The light was already starting to fade into dusk as the jury assembled in the dark interior of the cowshed. By this time the body was on its side, as it had been left by sorrowing relatives. But the crusted blood and the dark stain on the ground left little doubt as to the original position.

In preparing his report, Coroner Anderton noted the blood which had run from the nose and mouth. "There was dried blood on the shirt front which soaked through to the skin," he observed; "both hands were covered with dried blood. There was dried blood on the end of the penis for about an inch and a little on the right thigh below the groin." He also noted there was "no blood on the moccasins and only a small spot or two on the front of the overalls. There was none on the fly or on the buttons."[3]

After searching the area and finding no signs of a struggle,

38

Anderton arranged to have the body taken to the Big Bend detachment, where next morning the light would be good enough for Dr. Haultain to perform an autopsy. There was no doubt that Medicine Pipe Stem was dead, but how he had been killed, or even if he had been murdered, was still open to question.

Sleeps on Top, Yellow Creek, Red Crow, Young Pine, and a number of other Indians stood quietly around outside while the jury examined the body. Then, before the white men left for the police outpost, Yellow Creek called them aside. He was at last prepared to reveal what he had refused to divulge to Agent Wilson three days earlier.

He told about his brother's affair with Pretty Wolverine Woman and how Charcoal had found out about it. He told how, on the fateful day, his brother had followed the woman and her travois down towards the Belly River. That was the last time he had seen Medicine Pipe Stem alive. He was sure that Charcoal had done the killing.

On the basis of this information, Inspector Jarvis was prepared to bring Charcoal in — at least for questioning. As darkness was rapidly casting long shadows over the valley, this decision was put aside until morning. Then, while the autopsy was being performed at the detachment, the police would go to Bullhorn Coulee to arrest the suspect.

Chapter seven

During that entire day after Medicine Pipe Stem's body was found, Charcoal had stayed near his house, hoping that someone would bring news of McNeil's death. As the day wore on and no word was received, he became more and more worried. Anxiously he paced back and forth; he could not die until he knew that McNeil had already left for the spirit world. But the longer he waited, the more danger there was of being arrested. He didn't want to go to jail, in fact the very idea was unthinkable. He wanted only to shoot an important man, then kill his wife, and die.

As evening approached, Charcoal decided to find out what had happened. Saddling his buckskin horse, he called Pretty Wolverine Woman and told her to climb on behind him. If the news was good, they would not be coming back.

Several hours were spent aimlessly riding along the trail, past the school and over to Bullhorn Coulee, in the hope of meeting someone who had news of the shooting. He had to know. Pretty Wolverine Woman knew his intentions, just as she had for almost two weeks. During that time, she had lived in a state of almost numbing terror, afraid to stay yet more frightened at the thought of leaving. Her husband had remained close to her side the whole time, and she knew he would not hesitate to kill her. And if she fled, he might well destroy her children. On the other hand, she could not confide in anyone, because of the enormity of her own transgression in breaking tribal law. Deep down, she hoped that her husband might either change his mind or be quickly apprehended and her own life thus spared. Either way, she was not willing to make the first move. Now, she rode passively with the man who might soon become her murderer.

Long after dark, with still no news about McNeil, the worried Charcoal decided to flee. Fearful that the police would be watching his house, he took Pretty Wolverine Woman far out onto the prairie and left her there. She knew it was useless to run away, so she sat resignedly on the grass, awaiting his return.

At midnight Charcoal scouted around his camp and finally stopped in front of his cabin. His first action was to call his two step children outside and take them over to their grandmother's lodge where the rest of his family were.

"We are going away," he told the old woman,[1] indicating that she and Sleeping Woman were to come. When the grandmother protested, he threatened to kill the children. There was a tense pause. Then he ordered his daughter Owl Woman to prepare for the journey, and when she pleaded to stay, he threatened to kill her too. No one knew what had caused the strange transformation, but they all realized the man was deadly serious.

With no time to put on heavy clothes and only a few minutes to harness the horses, the silent party set out. Five were afraid to speak because of the smell of death in the air; the sixth had nothing to say. Charcoal led them south and some time later they reached his forlorn wife, cold and shivering in the chill of the October night. Now there were seven: Charcoal, his wives Pretty Wolverine Woman and Sleeping Woman, his mother-in-law Kills on Both Sides, his daughter Owl Woman, and his two step-children Bear Head and The Child.

Charcoal still had to find out what had happened to McNeil, so he decided to visit an old friend on Bullhorn Coulee — Young Pine, a longtime companion and the elder brother of his unfaithful wife. Leaving the frightened party on the edge of the coulee, he quietly went down the hill towards his friend's tepee. Riding his buckskin horse, Charcoal carried his Winchester across the saddle in front of him, while around his waist was fastened a full belt of cartridges.

Young Pine had returned from the murder scene upriver shortly after dark. The family knew that a killer was at large, and Yellow Creek's story about Pretty Wolverine Woman was already spreading across the reserve. Although he was a brave man, Young Pine was also prudent, so before he went to bed, he had told his wives, Hunchback and The Woman, to fasten the door flap and to tie an extra skin across the opening, on the inside. Yet they slept fitfully and soon heard the trotting horse and the creak of saddle leather. Young Pine's own horses whinnied to the stranger and milled restlessly as the buckskin drew near.

The tepee was in silence when Charcoal stopped before it, yet he knew the family was awake. In the moonlight, he could see where the wooden pins above the door had been removed so the occupants could peer outside.

"*Asoh'tokum.*" He called his friend's name. There was no reply. When the name was repeated Charcoal at last heard a stirring from within, and the flap was unfastened. Stepping inside, even in the darkness, he could sense they already knew about him. He was not just an ordinary fugitive, but one who had chosen to sacrifice his life and who could easily kill again.

"I have done wrong," he told them. "I have killed the boy upriver." No one ever called a recently deceased person by his real name, but this time, no explanation was needed. "I killed him because he was trying to take my wife away from me."[2] As he stood before the frightened trio, he told how the boy had looked up at him and how he had shot him through the eye.

Realizing the precariousness of the situation, Young Pine instructed one of his wives to make a fire and invited the visitor to eat. While they sat, Charcoal stated the reason for his visit. He told about his travels the night before and how he had fired at McNeil through the window of his house. "I am well satisfied with the shooting," he told his friend.[3]

Did Young Pine know about the farm instructor? Yes, he had heard the news. Was he dead? No, in fact the bullet had bounced off a plant in the window, and the man had suffered only a minor wound.

Charcoal sat silently for several minutes as though a sudden fear had gripped him. People knew about the murder, and he realized that soon the police would be looking for him. There was no point in killing his wife now; he first must have a chief to be his messenger to the spirit world. All he could do was to run and hide until he could find the right man.

At that moment the horses began stirring outside. Quickly Charcoal swung his rifle towards the door and slipped noiselessly outside. As soon as he was gone, Young Pine told his wives to gather up their two sleeping children, pull up the stakes at the back of the tepee, and hurry away to Eagle Child's place. Get help, he told them, so Charcoal can be captured before he kills anyone else.

Concerned about his sister, mother, and two nephews waiting on the hill, Young Pine saddled his horse and followed Charcoal to the rim of the coulee. There he kissed the terrified Pretty Wolverine Woman and his other relatives and, in hushed tones, told them about Medicine Pipe Stem and McNeil. In the meantime, Charcoal watched his family and friend with suspicion. Now there was no one he could trust; he could rely only on his religious powers and his Bear Knife to keep the police away.

Young Pine went to Charcoal and began speaking earnestly to him. His secret was safe, but if he ran away, everyone would know he was guilty. Eagle Shoe was suspected of killing Medicine Pipe Stem, and people thought the wounding of McNeil had something to do with a white man he had accidently killed a year earlier. At

42

first Charcoal rejected the stories but soon his wives and daughter were alongside Young Pine, saying that he told the truth. They were all cold and hungry and wanted to return to their cabin.

Reluctantly Charcoal acceded to their pleas and led them back towards the river. Cautiously he listened for any suspicious sounds; at one point he suddenly darted away towards a clump of brush near the dry coulee bottom. As Young Pine followed, Charcoal swung in his saddle, pointing his rifle at his brother-in-law's heart.

"You are lying to me!"

"No," replied Young Pine. "Even now people are saying it was a white man who shot McNeil. Come back with us!"[4]

Like a trapped animal, not knowing whom to trust, Charcoal held back until his friend rode beside him and gently pushed him forward — surreptitiously removing three cartridges from his belt as he did so. Still doubtful, Charcoal fell in behind the rest of the party until they reached the mouth of Bullhorn Coulee. There, once again, he wheeled away from the others, as though expecting a trap. But at last they reached the cabin, just a few hours before the first rays of light would streak the prairie sky.

The women were almost frozen as they scurried inside to light the stove. As they huddled around it, Charcoal entered the cabin and told Pretty Wolverine Woman to cook some food. Fearfully the family clustered near the stove, the women crying, afraid to run yet fearful of what would happen to them if they stayed. As the food was being prepared, Young Pine quietly suggested to the women that they overpower Charcoal, take his gun, and tie him up. After that, one of the boys could go for the police.

But Charcoal, ever suspicious, had already anticipated an attempt to trap him. His Winchester was not cradled in his arms as it had been earlier. He had hidden it, either inside the house or in the yard. If they jumped him and he tore free, he could get his gun and kill them all. And now that he had gone crazy they feared he would have the strength of a dozen men.

Just before sunrise, Charcoal became convinced that Young Pine had been lying to him. They were all waiting in the house for the police, and they were all telling him lies. Angrily he demanded that Pretty Wolverine Woman take down their tepee, which was pitched beside the cabin, and load their pack horses with food and supplies. When this had been done, he menacingly ordered Young Pine to leave and never to return. As he watched the frightened man lead his horse away, Charcoal recovered his rifle, and a few minutes later he rode backwards and forwards in front of the tiny assemblage of crying women and terrified children.

"If you don't come with me," he told them coolly, "I will kill all of you."[5]

There was no argument, only muffled sobs as the cavalcade slowly retraced its steps to Bullhorn Coulee and southwest towards the mountains. Keeping to the north to avoid Young Pine's place, they silently passed Running Crane's camp, crossed over the flats a few miles farther along, and picked up the well-worn trail.

Charcoal was in the lead. With his favorite buckskin horse beneath him and his rifle in front, he was like a warrior traveling through enemy country. At each bend in the coulee he rode cautiously forward, as though expecting an ambush. The rest of the time his eyes peered through the shadows of early morning which cast a gray pallor over the land. There was a flat dullness to the prairie that would vanish quickly, as soon as the sun burst forth over the eastern horizon.

There were no houses further along the coulee; the Bloods still followed the old tribal ways, camping close together near their favorite river bottoms. Usually they lived in family groups, just as they had in the buffalo days. Only a few of the more venturesome ones had wandered away to build ranches far from their home camps.

As the caravan plodded along the trail, the crying gradually ceased as the women accepted their fate. Owl Woman, the sixteen-year-old daughter of Charcoal, was the only exception. Fearful of what might happen to her and resentful because she had been drawn into a situation not of her own making, she continued to sob long after the others had stopped.

Finally Charcoal wheeled around, drew his Bear Knife from his belt, and brandished it in front of her face. Not a word was spoken, but the crying stopped.

The travelers came to a fork in the coulee and took the westerly trail towards Breastwork Hill just as the streaks of blue and purple in the sky gave way to the yellow rays of the sun. The shadows darted and scurried quickly through the grass as the gray of night retreated before the light of dawn. The flat land now became an undulating sea of short prairie wool, autumn browns interspersed with a few clumps of buckbrush and wild rose. In the coulees, dry washes showed where the waters ran in spring, and here and there, a large boulder or out-cropping of rock interrupted the brown monotony of grass.

Past Breastwork Hill, Charcoal led his family due south over a rise of land towards Lee's Creek. As they passed a low mound of rocks that marked the southern boundary of the Blood Reserve, Charcoal kept a sharp watch for white settlers. They were now only about eight miles straight west of Cardston, the Mormon village bordering the reserve. This area was densely populated with farmers, ranchers, and sheep herders.

Only a few good trails led through the steep canyon of Lee's Creek so there was no chance to remain hidden while the stream was being crossed. And as luck would have it, the last horse in the caravan had just stepped onto the south shore when a Mormon settler suddenly came into view. Leaving the others, Charcoal calmly rode forward to greet him. Using sign language, he told the white man that his family was going hunting in the mountains. The man nodded. Obviously he had heard nothing of the sensational events which were unfolding on the Blood Reserve. As a Mormon, he stayed with his own kind and let the Indians and Gentiles look after themselves. The meeting was of so little consequence that he had forgotten about the travelers before they had even left the valley.

Charcoal took his family up Lee's Creek for a couple of miles, until they reached its narrowest point. There he chose a campsite deep in the cottonwoods and willows, and told his wives to unpack. Then, while a small fire was lit and a meal prepared, Charcoal went to a nearby grass-covered hill to watch for any signs of pursuers.

That morning he had taken his family twenty-five miles from their cabin, through the sleeping reserve and into Mormon territory. No one would look for them there — at least not that day. He would now have a chance to think, to pray, and to decide what he would do next. This was not a good day to die.

Chapter eight

Damn!

A message arrived at Major Steele's office on Wednesday morning, 14 October, that all hell had broken out on the Blood Reserve. Inspector Jarvis and a small force of men had been on their way to arrest Charcoal, but as soon as they approached the mouth of Bullhorn Coulee, they had been surrounded by a bunch of excited Indians. In a matter of minutes they had learned that Charcoal and his family had fled but that Charcoal had first confessed. The stories were garbled, and there was as much gossip and speculation as there was real information, so it had taken the inspector some time to get the whole story.

It seemed that after Young Pine had been sent away from the cabin, he had gone directly to Big Snake's house. Arousing his friend from bed, he had told him that Charcoal was crazy and was keeping his family imprisoned in his house. Afraid to take on the man without reinforcements, Big Snake had gone to the Fish Eaters' camp to get help from Sleeps on Top and Crop Eared Wolf. At the same time, Young Pine had headed towards Bullhorn Coulee to arouse Packs His Tail and to see if his wives had alerted Eagle Child. Once assembled, they had found there were only one rifle and a revolver among the six of them, but they had decided to go over to Charcoal's place anyway. There they had discovered the house empty and all the horses gone.

Parties were already searching through the brush along the river bottom when Inspector Jarvis appeared. They were sure Charcoal was hiding somewhere nearby. In the meantime, Young Pine had gone to the Indian Agency where he told about the confession which he had heard and how Charcoal claimed to have shot the young Indian through the eye.

Now this was real news! Not even the coroner had discovered how Medicine Pipe Stem had died. That very day the police surgeon would be conducting an autopsy to determine the cause of death. Steele had little doubt about what he would find.

46

Damn!

Already the police had one fugitive at large in the Saskatchewan country. A full year had passed since Almighty Voice had shot down the Mounted Police sergeant, and questions were being asked about the efficiency of the force. Newspapers wanted to know if the police were losing control in the North West and why the famous riders of the plains could not locate one renegade Indian.

Earlier in the year a suggestion had been made that the Canadian Militia might be expanded into the west "to utilize the guns lying idle at the Police posts."[1] The implication had been clear. Then a judge in Halifax had told two convicted burglars that they would be set free if they agreed to join the Mounted Police. The western press had reacted quickly to this slander and risen to defend the force against "injustice and misrepresentation at the hands of eastern newspapers."[2] But the detractors were not to be silenced. A short time later, another critic had suggested that the Mounted Police be reduced by 100 men and their places be taken by volunteers.

To make matters worse, a general election had been held only three months earlier, and after eighteen years in office with a succession of lackluster prime ministers, the Conservative party had been soundly defeated. In its place, the Liberals had won a decisive victory under the capable leadership of Wilfrid Laurier.

Although Steele was not really a political appointee, he had received his important commissions from Conservative governments; all of them had been approved by Sir John A. Macdonald himself. But more important, Steele knew that for several years before they assumed office the Liberals had been attacking the police and had even recommended that the force be abolished. Laurier himself on one occasion had said that "the force was not established to remain permanent and perennial. It was understood that one day it should cease."[3]

Now, with the Liberal's first session of Parliament in progress, another Indian had committed murder, wounded a white man, and eluded the police.

In order to prevent the prime minister from hearing about the trouble through the Toronto *Globe* or, worse, through a question from the opposition, Major Steele wired his superiors in Ottawa, urging them to let Laurier know what had happened. Obligingly, the force's commissioner passed on the message.

"I am informed by telegraph," he told the prime minister, "that the body of an Indian supposed to have been murdered has been found on the Blood Reserve near Macleod, and that the Coroner is investigating. Also that an Indian fired at and slightly

47

wounded one of the white men employed on the . . . reservation on the night of the 12th, and that investigation is now going on.

"I do not anticipate anything serious from these reports, and merely advise you in order that you may be able to appreciate the value of anything you may see in the newspapers on the subject."[4]

He was none too early with this information, for the local correspondents to the *Manitoba Free Press* and Winnipeg *Daily Tribune* had already been busy. As soon as the *Free Press* stringer heard the first rumors, he wired a confused account of Medicine Pipe Stem's death, alleging that McNeil had been shot while trying to prevent the murder. He claimed that the farm instructor was dangerously wounded.

On Wednesday he telegraphed another story saying "there is apparently no connection between the two crimes, the murder of the Indian and the shooting of McNeil."[5] But the next day he had another correction to make. This time he reported that "in connection with the murder of an Indian and the attempt to shoot Instructor McNeil, it turns out the same Indian who committed the murder attempted the killing of Mr. McNeil by shooting through the window. It is reported here this morning he has since murdered his squaw and child. He is armed and is hiding in the brush."[6]

Then in a classic reaffirmation of the myth that the Mountie "always gets his man," the local stringer added, "Major Steele will not be stood off. He never has been and never will be."[7]

The eastern press, always looking for a good wild-west story, picked up the Winnipeg releases, and soon such headlines as "Terror of the Plains,"[8] "The Bad Indian,"[9] and "Indian Kills Another"[10] were appearing in the Montreal *Star*, Toronto *Globe*, and other papers. They too put their faith in the Mounted Police officer: the *Globe* reported that Charcoal "is well provided with ammunition and arms, and is defying the police, but Major Steele says he will capture him."[11]

After seeing to it that the prime minister was warned about the situation, Steele wired the news to the Indian agent on the Blackfoot reservation in Montana, just south of the line. The Indians on that reservation spoke the same language as the Bloods and were part of the same nation. Many had relatives on both sides of the border and were constantly visiting back and forth. If Charcoal got over there, the whole process of extradition would probably take months.

Meanwhile, Inspector Jarvis and his men had joined the Indians who were searching the river bottom, convinced that a party of seven would have been seen if it had tried to flee the area. The manhunt was still underway when Dr. Haultain arrived from upriver with the body of Medicine Pipe Stem in the back of a wagon. Because the search was now being coordinated out of Standoff, he had chosen to take the body there for the autopsy, rather than stay at the Big Bend outpost.

It did not take him long to confirm the cause of death. "On sponging & opening the eyes," he wrote in his notes, "found a small penetrating wound on left eye ball, the lids being intact except for slight tearing near inner corner. . . . The direction of the wound was downwards, breaking into fragments."[12] The bullet had passed through the roof of the mouth, broken the man's jaw from the inside, and deflected straight down through his heart. After three days of police investigations, the bullet wound had finally been found, and it was all as Young Pine had said. No real doubt remained as to the killer's identity. When the coroner's jury assembled, it concurred that Medicine Pipe Stem had been killed by a bullet supposedly fired by Charcoal.

The timing of this trouble couldn't have been worse for Sam Steele. Although he was superintendent for "D" Division of the North West Mounted Police, he was also aware of the potential for wealth through investment in the West. This was a new country, and if a man were lucky enough to be on hand when discoveries were being made, he might do very well for himself.

In 1887 and 1888, Steele had taken his division into the wilds of British Columbia to settle a dispute between the Kootenay Indians and the miners. Camping near the Wildhorse gold diggings, he had erected a post, which was naturally named Fort Steele. After a year matters had settled down sufficiently for him to return to the prairies, but during his months in the mountains, he had become interested in mining ventures and had watched for opportunities which might pay handsome dividends.

Although mineral deposits were known to exist in the west Kootenay area, the district was isolated from the Canadian Pacific by miles of lakes and mountains. The single rail line south to Spokane was an asset, but the cost of shipping raw ore was still prohibitive. Now, in 1896, all this was changing, for a British mining syndicate had bought claims on Toad Mountain and was building a large smelter to process ore for the entire district.

The resulting mining craze spread all across Canada but was particularly strong among the merchants and residents of southern Alberta. During the summer, Steele and a number of friends contacted a mining engineer, William Tretheway, and arranged to buy four claims in the boom area. These were the Ibex, Triangle, Gilt Edge, and Liddlesdale properties, which contained good showings of galena. Tests made by Tretheway revealed a vein of ore ranging from nine to nineteen inches in width, averaging eighty-five ounces of silver and sixty-seven percent lead in a 300-foot cut.

As soon as word was out that Major Steele was forming a company, a number of his fellow policemen were ready to invest. "We had faith," recalled Supt. R. B. Deane of Lethbridge, "and we backed our faith with good dollar bills. . . . A banker calculated that a sum of at least one hundred thousand dollars had been withdrawn from circulation in Macleod and Lethbridge. Superintendent Sam Steele . . . was the mainspring of the movement, and that was a guarantee that the conduct of the business was at least honest."[13]

Among those investing, besides Deane, were Insp. G. E. Sanders of Macleod, Inspector Jarvis at Big Bend, and S. Sgt. Chris Hilliard at Standoff. These men, with a few Macleod merchants, paid $3,000 down on a $30,000 bond for the properties and hired seven men to build cabins, open trails, and prepare for full-scale mining operations in the fall.

As a result, the major had his hands full when the news came about Charcoal's flight. He was just completing plans to incorporate the new group as the Ibex Mining and Development Company, of which he would be president, and was arranging to have equipment shipped into the area via Spokane. As a matter of fact, he had been setting out to see the customs officials when the news had arrived.

Clearly, his investment would have to wait; he must mobilize his men to find Charcoal. After the proper authorities in Ottawa and Regina had been notified about the murder, Steele dispatched Sgt. W. B. Macleod to Standoff with seven men; they were to help in the search. Then he notified Insp. A. R. Cuthbert at Pincher Creek to be on guard. With this done, he set aside his mining plans and prepared to go to Standoff himself, so he could personally supervise the manhunt. He would leave first thing in the morning.

That night, Indian guards were posted all along the Belly River in case Charcoal should return. To them, he was now the *enemy*, a coyote-crazy renegade who was capable of killing either friend or foe. No one knew if his family was alive or dead, and, with nothing to lose, he might appear out of the darkness to kill again.

Red Crow, who was a special target for the fugitive, took to sleeping on the floor. Charcoal had been in his house many times and knew where his bed was situated; some night he could easily smash the window and kill him. The chief was also afraid that Charcoal might take revenge on his family, so he sent word to the Dunbow Indian school, asking them to guard his son who was a pupil there.

50

The chief's fears were shared by many others on the reserve. Doors were locked at night, tepees were fastened, and anyone who owned a gun kept it nearby. White Calf, who had been a great war chief in his younger years, climbed into his loft each evening and drew his ladder up behind him.

None of the Bloods could argue with the Indian agent's description of Charcoal as "a very quiet inoffensive person and about the last Indian on the Reserve one would think likely to commit such a crime."[14] But that was before he decided to abandon his life. Now he was like some maddened beast, prowling through the night, capable of killing without rhyme or reason. To make matters worse, the Bloods knew that Charcoal still had his supernatural powers. He was the owner of the Bear Knife, which gave him the savagery and strength of the grizzly. He was a member of the Horn Society and a medicine-pipe owner, each of which gave him certain undefinable and unexplainable powers. The nights would be long and fearful while Charcoal was at large.

After Steele had made the twenty-mile drive from Macleod to Standoff next morning, he held long sessions with Agent Wilson and Inspector Jarvis to get a firsthand account of the events. The official findings of the coroner's jury were also passed on to him so that a warrant could be issued for Charcoal's arrest.

The search of the Belly River valley had produced nothing, so arrangements were made through the Indian agent for six scouts to extend the search along the nearby Waterton River. These half-dozen men were an addition to the regular complement of Indian Department and Mounted Police scouts who were already taking part in the search. With Cliff Clarke, the farm instructor, in charge, the six armed Bloods were to start at the mouth of the Waterton and work their way upstream to the mountains. Though Major Steele looked for the co-operation of the Indians throughout the operation, he did not entirely trust these warlike tribesmen. "There were not more than thirty armed by us at any one time," he assured the Mounted Police commissioner, "and the quantity of ammunition issued was small."[15]

Yet Steele had no reason to worry, for the Bloods were as anxious as the police to capture Charcoal. The major interpreted the case as a simple love triangle that had resulted in murder, causing the culprit to run amok. But the Indians realized that Charcoal had chosen his own violent pathway to the spirit world and that as long as he was alive no one would be safe.

This, then, was at the heart of the whole tragic affair. Charcoal, only two decades removed from unrestrained freedom, had no concept of the white man's justice. He knew only that killing was not permitted and that a killer would be hanged. He had broken the white man's law so his life was finished. Major Steele, on the other hand, was the product of generations of military life. His father had been a captain in the Royal Navy, his great-uncle a colonel in the army, and his maternal great-grand-father a British captain. His ancestors had been present with Lord Nelson in his naval battles and at the capture of Quebec. The major himself had joined the militia at the time of the Fenian raids and had taken part in the Red River expedition. To him, British law and British justice were not mere phrases, but a way of life.

It is unlikely that Steele could have fully understood Charcoal's motivations. Spirit worlds, ghost messengers, and supernatural powers were all foreign to his well-disciplined life. A devout Anglican, he saw many native traditions as simple superstitions which prevented the Indians from becoming "civilized." That Charcoal should react differently than a European in any given situation or that he would fail to put the right interpretation on the Queen's law was probably incomprehensible to him.

Steele saw nothing incongruous in Charcoal's transformation into a daring outlaw. There was a simple explanation: the Indian agent who had described him as a quiet and inoffensive man was obviously wrong. In his scenario, Steele cast the fugitive as a lifelong renegade who had once been "one of their most remarkable young warriors, a hero in their eyes from every point of view. In those days he rarely slept in his camp, was generally on the warpath or on horse stealing expeditions against the hereditary enemies of his tribe, a restless brave who for a long time hated the whites."[16] His reason for trying to kill McNeil and fleeing from the reserve, according to Steele, was that he "was determined to leave a name which would not soon be forgotten."[17]

In the European world, only such a man would have reacted the way Charcoal did; there was no need to probe more deeply or to be concerned with native superstitions. The fugitive was a desperate, cunning warrior who had reverted to type and now had to be hunted down. Then he would be tried and convicted, the British way.

Chapter nine

After Charcoal chose the campsite on Lee's Creek early on the fourteenth, he stayed on the hillside all day, keeping an eye on his family below and watching the nearby trails for signs of his pursuers. At sunset he went back to the camp where he told Pretty Wolverine Woman to pitch their tepee. Soon it would be dark enough so that no one could see it in the dense timber.

After he had eaten he told his family all that had happened. He gave details about the planned sweat lodge, how he had discovered his wife with Medicine Pipe Stem in the cowshed, and how he had shot him in the head. He also admitted that he had fired at Farmer McNeil through the agency window.

Now, for the first time, the entire family knew what had happened. The few whispered remarks from Young Pine during the night had made them realize that the trouble was serious, but now they understood why Charcoal had threatened them and why, like a warrior, he carried his Bear Knife in his belt rather than wrapped in its sacred bundle.

They were only about six miles from the international boundary; a half-hour's journey would take them out of the reach of Major Steele and his red coats. But Charcoal made no move in that direction; he chose instead to stay in the land he knew so well. In the ensuing days, he never wandered more than thirty miles from his home and was usually within sight of the massive Chief Mountain.

Next morning, just before sunrise, Charcoal awakened his family, and soon they were off again. "We are going to the Pine Timber," he told them.[1] Crossing the creek they followed the steep foothills west along the base of the mountains until they reached the main trail between the Blood Reserve and the timber limit. Swinging south, they followed along the Belly River for about four miles to a narrow canyon which marked the entrance to the 4,000 acres of forest which had been set aside for the Blood tribe.

53

A little further along, they came to a deep hollow surrounded on three sides by heavy timber and almost within the shadow of Chief Mountain; there Charcoal indicated they would make their camp. The women nervously unpacked the horses, carefully piling the folded tepee, flour, sugar, tea, and other essentials which would enable them to stay in hiding for weeks. Charcoal then took the horses some distance away to let them graze.

In the late afternoon, he announced that he was going away by himself for awhile. He would not be back until late, he said, and warned his family not to run away. No one argued, for they were too many to travel without mounts. He told his wife to pitch the tepee after dark and await his return.

Walking up the slope to the flat above, Charcoal noted with satisfaction how well the camp was hidden from any casual passerby. All he could see were the tall pines and the heavy growth of willows and underbrush.

Roping his buckskin horse, the man was soon on his way, leading a packhorse behind him. Carefully he scouted the Blood Reserve trail, following it out of the mountains and into the lake-dotted foothills. Sighting a small herd of range cattle, he watched it until nightfall to be sure no riders were around. Then, moving cautiously like a raider creeping into an enemy camp, he singled out a steer, killed it, and quickly butchered it on the spot. When the meat was loaded on the packhorse, he silently faded back into the mountains. Later, when his wife unloaded the meat, he discovered he had lost the kidney on the trail. This was sad news, for fresh kidney was a delicacy to be eaten raw. With a sigh, Charcoal told the women to leave the meat until morning when there would be light to butcher it properly.

The next day, 16 October, was a busy one. Pretty Wolverine Woman and Kills on Both Sides set to work to cut the meat and prepare it for drying. Charcoal had been restless all night, and as the women worked he stood beside them, repeating the story of his wife's infidelity, the murder of Medicine Pipe Stem, and the shooting of McNeil. Then, in deep despair, he walked to the top of the ridge to gaze out over the valley. Finally, singing his warrior's song he wept in anguish, in agony. Faced with certain death, he had chosen to flee rather than to travel to the spirit world unannounced. Now there was no point in killing his wife, nor any of his family, because he still had no ghostly messenger. Tired, sick, and frightened, he cried — a man alone, with nothing before him but darkness. His wailing was heard by the family below, and when he returned, he was surprised to see his daughter weeping also.

"Father, I wish I could kill her," she sobbed, looking toward the apprehensive Pretty Wolverine Woman. "She's the cause of all our misfortune. You've been a good husband to her, but she never appreciated your kindness. Let me kill her."

"My child," he told Owl Woman, "you mustn't talk so. I know what's going to happen to me. But you're still young; you must go on with your life."[2]

Late in the afternoon, Charcoal went out to check his horses again, then scouted the area for signs of intruders. Hearing a noise downstream, he cautiously led his buckskin along the trail until the sound of someone chopping wood separated itself from the rippling waters, the chattering of magpies, and the rustling of the autumn wind through the tall pines. Tying his horse in a dense growth of trees, Charcoal crept close enough to see a white man trimming poles and loading them onto a wagon. Some distance away, his coat had been tossed to one side as he struggled with his load.

Until this time, Charcoal had been careful to hide his trail and to stay out of sight. Yet he knew when he had run away, that, unthinkingly, he had taken on the traditional role of the rabid coyote and could draw supernatural wisdom from that animal. Among the Bloods, a man who cared nothing for his life, but was ready to throw it away, was like the crazy coyote, an unpredictable animal which would chase its own tail while food lay nearby. It would hide from those who could kill it, then defiantly go out to attack them.

This was the creature which Charcoal had chosen to imitate when he had decided to flee from the reserve. Now, completely disregarding all his previous efforts to remain hidden, he began to act out the role which circumstances had thrust upon him. Jumping suddenly to his feet, he rushed across the clearing and grabbed the woodcutter's coat. The man saw him, of course, and tried to catch him, but the fugitive was quickly out of sight in the trees.

As he returned to camp, Charcoal remembered a song that was meant for people like him.

Oh, coyotes are crazy,
They catch what they want,
Hai, ya, hai ya, ho![3]

This song was now a part of Charcoal's life, and like his medicine bundles, prayers, and supernatural powers, it placed him in a strange land somewhere between the material and spiritual worlds. He was surrounded not only by hostile white men who would come looking for him, but by a host of mystical forces which could help him or destroy him.

Charcoal's world had always been filled with ghosts, spirits, and the supernatural. An unusual rock on the prairie or a twisted tree at the entrance to a mountain pass was believed to possess strange powers. No one could ever be sure if they were good or bad, so a small offering was left — just in case.

The bottoms of rivers and lakes were inhabited by underwater people who could assist a man or ruin him. It was the underwater people who gave the Blackfoot the beaver bundle, the oldest ceremonial object in the nation. According to tradition, it had come from Saint Mary's Lake, only a few miles from where Charcoal was camped. A hunter whose marksmanship was so good that he was killing all the game was asked by the spirits to stop. When he agreed, the underwater people gave him the beaver bundle and taught him the songs that went with it. That has happened generations ago, long before the Bloods saw their first horses.

Two other men, Weasel Heart and Most Sacred Man, had actually gone to visit the underwater people and had been given two painted tepees. These were the yellow and black buffalo lodges, each with its own special songs, ceremonies, and powers.

But sometimes the underwater people were evil. There was one instance in which two starving Indians found the body of a monster washed up on the shore of a stream. When one of them ate its flesh, he was turned into an underwater creature.

The sky, too, was a separate land. It was governed by the Sun, his wife the Moon, and their boy the Morning Star. Everyone in the tribe knew how Morning Star had married a girl from earth and taken her to the sky land. She was very happy, and by the time their union was blessed with a child, she had forgotten the world below. Then, one day, she ignored the warnings of her husband and pulled a huge wild turnip which was growing in the celestial land. Through the hole that it left, she could see through the clouds to the earth below; suddenly she was homesick and unhappy.

Realizing that his wife could no longer stay in the sky, Morning Star instructed her to cut a long rope from a buffalo skin so that she could lower herself to earth. Before she left, she was taught the songs and ceremonies which would allow her people to proclaim their faith in the Sun. And so it was that the Sun Dance came to the prairies. Charcoal knew all about it, for as a young boy he had been painted by the holy ones and taught how to cut the rawhide for the Sun Dance lodge, just as the woman had cut the rope countless years before.

And there was a land of the dead. This, too, was a real place in the Sand Hills on the eastern edge of their hunting grounds. When a man died, his spirit would stay around for a while, sometimes causing trouble and striking fear in those who were still alive. The place where he died became his spirit dwelling, and if it was comfortable the ghost might stay there for months. That was why the Bloods often moved a dying man into his tepee, for after his death the canvas could be folded up so that the ghost would have no place to stay. If a man did happen to die in his cabin, it was abandoned and eventually torn down.

They were always careful to dress the dying man well and to place his belongings beside him, for these would become ghost objects which he could take to the Sand Hills. Often a horse was killed nearby so that he might ride into the land of the dead.

Once the spirit decided to leave its place of death, he would travel eastward to seek the ghostly villages. There, as in life, he would have his own tepee, horses, and other property. The only difference was that the spirit became a tiny shadow, hunting mice which now seemed as big as the shaggy buffalo.

The Bloods knew much about the dead, for some of the medicine men were able to speak to the spirits. One man, a Blackfoot, even went to that strange land and returned.

It happened many years ago. When the man's wife died he became so lonely that he decided to search for her. He traveled for four days and four nights to the east, until he met a strange boy, only a shadow and a voice. After the Blackfoot had explained his mission, the ghost led him to a lone tepee in the Sand Hills where he was told to sit in the place of honor. There he could hear voices but could see nothing until a stone pipe was lit by the boy and passed around. As each ghost smoked, its arms appeared; the second time they smoked their chests came into view; the third time the man could see their knees; and the fourth time their whole bodies appeared.

When the ghostly council learned why the Indian had come to the land of the dead, they gathered together all the recent arrivals at the village, but his wife was not among them.

"There are four camps of lodges in the Sand Hills," explained the ghost. "The next is beyond here, the third farther away, and the fourth beyond that one."[4]

Traveling to the second and third villages, the man faced further disappointment, but at the fourth, he was overjoyed to see his wife standing with the crowd. Warned not to touch her, the Indian was given a stone pipe and instructed how to use it. The pipe was placed on the woman's back, and the man was told, to walk ahead of her without looking back.

Four days later they came to a hill overlooking his home camp. As a rider came up to greet them, he was told to prepare four sweat lodges. When the man and woman entered the first one to purify themselves, they left behind a disgusting scattering of dead vermin, snakes, manure, and sand. After the second sweat lodge there were fewer remains, fewer still after the third, and none after

57

the fourth. The couple was now purified and returned to a normal life in their tribe. The land of the dead had not only given up one of its people, but a ghost medicine pipe as well.

There were many such stories which Charcoal knew. Even at the time he was in hiding, there was a minor chief in his tribe named Calf Shirt who had been to the Sand Hills. When there Calf Shirt had met a snake spirit who had given him the power to handle rattlesnakes and to treat them as his children. It was said that when he died, Calf Shirt would go to the spirit world of the snakes to become one of them, rather than to the ghost villages.

So death for Charcoal was simply a transfer to a spirit world where he would have his own lodge, his horses, and shadowy friends. Yet there were risks. If he were killed by the Mounted Police, they might put him in a box and bury him in the ground, just as the missionaries did. If that happened, he believed his spirit would be trapped forever in the land of the underground people. Yes, even the underground ones had their own separate land.

The missionaries had been with the Bloods for almost twenty years, yet no one would willingly let a relative be buried underground. If they had a choice, they would have him wrapped in blankets and placed in the forks of a tree or sewn up in his lodge on a lonely hill. On the other hand, if the missionary influence was strong, the family might build a tiny house, large enough to hold the coffin but open so that the spirit could leave whenever it wished. Such ghost houses were built in isolated coulees or on hilltops where they provided a dwelling which would probably keep the spirit around for many months, perhaps years.

A man like Charcoal did not want to take chances with any of these innovations which might trap his spirit. He agreed with his young wife's father, the war chief Medicine Calf, who said to his friends before his death, "Bury me not in the ground like a white man, I am an Indian. Lay me down as an Indian warrior, and there let me rest."[5]

Chapter ten

On Friday, 16 October, Major Steele ordered Inspector Jarvis to take a party of police and Indians west up the Belly River to continue the search. That night they were to meet with Steele and Farmer Clarke's patrol at Spring Hill and continue towards the mountains on the following day. These arrangements made, the major drove south to Cardston where he dispatched Insp. H. J. A. Davidson and a constable to patrol up Lee's Creek and meet the other parties in the mountains. With the sun still high in the afternoon sky, Steele then circled around the southern tip of the Blood Reserve to the Big Bend detachment. There he again met Jarvis and learned that the patrols had so far found nothing.

The first break came later that evening when a settler named James Henderson rode into the detachment looking for the police. He was unaware of the manhunt that was taking place, but a short time earlier he had been loading timber near the mountains when an Indian had stolen his overcoat. The incident had taken place just a few miles from the Blood timber limit on the upper waters of the Belly River, and the thief fitted the description of the wanted man.

By this time, Clarke's Indians and Jarvis's patrol were camped close to Big Bend; from there they could approach the timber limit from the north. Inspector Davidson, reinforced by two men from the Boundary Creek outpost, was patrolling the Canada-United States border and would be approaching the timber limit from the south. There was only one trail into the mountainous area, so if the fugitive was there he was trapped. To prepare for the attack Inspector Jarvis and his men were sent off that night to establish a rendezvous point on West's ranch, at the edge of the mountains.

Early Saturday morning, the Mounted Police and Indian scouts gathered at the entrance to the timber limit. It was the middle of October, and though the weather was still warm and dry, the brisk mountain air gave promise that winter was not far off.

The scouts had been up all night on the side of the mountain, waiting for dawn. As the first rays of sun crept over the ragged line of trees, the Indians peered down towards the timber limit. Gradually they could see the hills, the valleys, and the upland pastures where elk liked to graze in winter. When the light reflected off the water of the Belly River, Yellow Bull saw something moving. Training his field glasses on the spot, he made out two pinto horses, facing each other neck to neck; behind them was the pale haze of campfire smoke.

"That's him!" exclaimed Yellow Bull. "That's Charcoal."[1]

Back at the base camp, the scouts reported their discovery just as the sun was clearing the eastern horizon. Major Steele had decided not to take part in the raid; he would remain behind at the Big Bend detachment, from which point he could plan strategy and direct the campaign. That left Jarvis in command at the rendezvous camp.

Under instructions from Jarvis, the men divided into small parties of four or five, with the police taking off their high leather boots so they could travel as silently as their Indian scouts. Their hats were removed as well, so that the noise of a branch brushing against the stiff fabric would not alert the fugitive.

"I was in the party to the extreme right," recalled Const. Joe Gillespie years later, "and after creeping cautiously through the brush for several miles in the direction ordered by the Inspector we came to the brink of a deep ravine or coulee. From out of the trees a way down at the bottom of this coulee floated a haze of blue smoke. Looking closer we could discern a tepee."[2]

All was quiet around the camp, and even though it was about ten o'clock there was no sign of anyone wandering around. The hollow, about 500 acres in size, was filled with dense pine and underbrush six feet high. It was not possible to descend directly into it, for the noise of the men struggling down the slopes would have aroused the entire camp. Instead, a number of the police and scouts were sent to an old creek bed some distance away, with instructions to follow it down towards the lodge. Others went in the opposite direction where they found another way of reaching the lower ground. The remainder were posted along the edge of the coulee in case the outlaw came that way.

As the patrols approached the silent camp, someone stepped on a dry branch, and the crack echoed like thunder in the tiny valley. Charcoal was out of the lodge in an instant, his Winchester in hand. Without a moment's hesitation Green Grass opened fire, and his shot was followed by a veritable fusilade of bullets. Yellow Bull took careful aim at Charcoal, and when he missed, he fired another eleven shots "at nothing in particular."[3] Charcoal was only twenty feet from the closest rifleman, but he miraculously evaded their shots, dashed around the tepee, and dived into the brush. As he disappeared into the thick trees, he was singing his Bear Knife song. Meanwhile, to encourage the attackers, one of the scouts shouted in Blackfoot, "*Poksapot*! He's alone! What are you afraid of?"[4]

The women and children, terrified by the flying bullets, burst from the lodge one by one. Green Grass, who was closest, managed to grab the mother-in-law, Kills on Both Sides, and one of the stepchildren as they tried to rush by. Constable Gillespie, who was down in the campsite moments later, found a badly frightened Owl Woman still cowering inside. The others had followed Charcoal into the trees.

The camp looked as though the occupants had been prepared for a long stay — a sack of flour, meat hanging to dry, and quantities of food and clothing sufficient to keep them for at least two months. Had the snows come early, they probably could have maintained this isolated retreat as long as Charcoal wanted to stay; instead, he had chosen to play the part of a crazy coyote and reveal himself to the white man.

The lightning raid had resulted in the capture of Charcoal's entire horse herd, his painted tepee, and all his possessions except his rifle and ammunition. Inside the lodge, hanging from a cord, he had even abandoned his Bear Knife in his flight to freedom.

Inspector Jarvis realized that Charcoal couldn't get far afoot, so he immediately sent one party under Sergeant Macleod to search the brush as far as the river bottom and another under S. Sgt. Chris Hilliard to go upstream.

As one of the searchers, Constable Gillespie, later pointed out, "Beating around in the brush with the knowledge that at any moment you may be surprised and your body made the lodging place for a bullet is not at any time a very pleasant occupation, and was most certainly not on this occasion as we knew that our quarry was desperate and would not hesitate to shoot on sight."[5]

When no signs of the fugitive could be found, Jarvis extended the manhunt to the entire width of brush in the Belly River valley. At this point, Staff Sergeant Hilliard noticed Inspector Davidson and his party coming downstream from Chief Mountain, having just crossed Belly River Pass. Unaware of the events which had taken place, Davidson's patrol had unknowingly cut off any escape toward the United States border.

Signaling them with a mirror, Hilliard brought the patrol over to the rest of the party to let them know about the morning raid. Davidson then continued downstream to Jarvis's rendezvous camp outside the mountains and swung southeast along the foothills to Bright's abandoned ranch. This, reasoned the officer, would allow him to intercept Charcoal and his family should they try to make their way over the tree-covered mountain and toward the Blood Reserve. From the ranch he sent two men to patrol the international boundary, while he remained on guard with Constable Nettleship.

That night, Jarvis placed guards on all the vantage points along the Belly River near the timber limit, while Davidson's men watched the boundary and the eastern slopes. No one had seen the fugitive since the raid; he seemed to have disappeared into thin air.

Yet Charcoal's movements should have been predictable. As soon as the shooting had broken out he had dashed into the trees without firing a shot. In fact, except for Green Grass, he had barely seen his attackers. Dropping behind some fallen timber, he had collected his terror-stricken wives, Pretty Wolverine Woman and Sleeping Woman, and his stepson as they had hurried toward him. After the shooting had stopped and while the police were rounding up their prisoners, he had guided the escapees away from the coulee into thick timber, where they had sat quietly until nightfall. Pretty Wolverine Woman had had no wish to stay with her husband, but she had found no opportunity to escape during the melee. At the sound of gunfire, her first reaction had been to flee; unfortunately her route led her right into the arms of her coyote-crazy mate.

Although he had lost his Bear Knife, Charcoal was convinced that it had given him the power to escape. If ever a knife owner was trapped by an enemy, all he had to do was to sing the Bear Knife song, and the trap would spring open. It was said that even if a man were wearing handcuffs, they would spring loose halfway through the song.

After the night-shadows had blanketed the valley, Charcoal led his captive family due east over the tree-clad mountain which was known to the whites as Pole Heaven, because of the excellent stand of lodgepole pine. On the other side he knew there were several small ranches where he might be able to find some horses and, without realizing that Davidson's patrol was waiting for him, he decided to visit the Bright ranch first.

"The horses ridden by Constable Nettleship and myself were pretty well played out," Inspector Davidson ruefully reported later to Major Steele, "having been travelling the previous night, and throughout the day. I decided to put them in the stable at the ranch, and to go out on foot into the bush with Nettleship to watch for Charcoal."[6]

Two hours later, his family riding double on the two Mounted Police horses stolen from the stable, Charcoal set out for the

United States border. As he approached the line, he swung into the heavy timber on the nearby slopes, knowing that it would be impossible to track him through this kind of terrain. Then he turned north again for the rolling hills beyond the Belly River. He was free!

Major Steele was astounded when the news of the attack began to filter back to him. First came the heartening word that two women and a boy had been captured. Then he learned that Charcoal had escaped, even though surrounded by more than two dozen armed men. He had fled unscathed, while one of the police had suffered a minor injury: in the confusion, a bullet had creased Inspector Jarvis's hairline and sent his cap flying through the air.

With a search underway in the dense brush, Steele hoped it would only be a matter of time before Charcoal and the other three were caught. Then, as the disheartening hours passed, the major anxiously sent a messenger galloping to the Blood Agency, asking Wilson to send another thirty Indians to help in the hunt.

Next morning, the unwelcome news about Charcoal's horse raid on Bright's ranch reached Major Steele at about five o'clock when a shamefaced Inspector Davidson arrived at Big Bend to announce that his animals had been stolen, complete with saddles and a pair of binoculars.

Raging that the officer had "committed a great error of judgement in leaving his horses without a guard,"[7] Steele sent his Indian scouts and Staff Sergeant Hilliard back to the ranch, where they followed the tracks into the brush near Boundary Creek. Reporting back to Big Bend, they told the major that Charcoal's trail was last seen heading due south only a couple of miles from the United States boundary. His raid on the ranch had taken place several hours earlier, so he could be all the way south to Cutbank or Two Medicine Creek in Montana among the lodges and cabins of the South Peigans. With a number of his relatives living down there, he would have no difficulty in finding someone to hide him.

In the meantime, the agent, reacting quickly to Steele's request for help, had visited every village along the river, urging able-bodied Indians with horses to meet him at the house of Bull Horn, a minor chief. From there, they had been led upriver by a Mounted Police constable and the Indian agent, toward Big Bend and the scene of the battle.

The Bloods were excited and ready for the hunt. During the past few days, more and more Indians had abandoned their small, unprotected ranches for the comparative security of tepee camps at the Upper and Lower Agencies. It was just like in the old buffalo days when they had learned that an enemy was near. Each night they tethered their best horses nearby, sealed their doorways, and listened fearfully for night sounds which might reveal a stranger's presence.

They did not like to feel so helpless and afraid, so when the chance came to put an end to Charcoal's freedom, the Bloods volunteered willingly. This was not done to please the Mounted Police, nor to help the white man; it was simply a matter of self-preservation. They did not hate Charcoal; they feared him for what he had become.

Only his brothers and others in the Choking band refused to support the search. Although shocked by Charcoal's action, their anger was directed towards Pretty Wolverine Woman, who had shamed them all by having an affair with a blood relative. The murder had been justified, they felt; Charcoal's wife was the one who had driven him to commit his warlike deeds. He was still their brother, and while the members of the band had often been derided for their internal squabbling, they always seemed to unite against a common enemy.

When the Bloods assembled by Agent Wilson were still several miles from Big Bend, a messenger met them with the news that Charcoal had escaped. His trail led south, so he was probably already in Montana. All the same, the entire contingent was to be pressed into service in the search. By this time, some of the other Indian scouts had already been scouring the area for an entire day, and Green Grass complained that they "worked so hard that their moccasins wore out and they had to borrow handkerchiefs to bind their feet."[8]

The manhunt had become a fiasco. First the patrol had missed Charcoal at his cabin on the Blood Reserve by a matter of hours. Then the police had him surrounded with a couple of dozen armed men, yet he had escaped in broad daylight with his two wives and boy. Not only that, he had now eluded their dragnet and fled on two Mounted Police horses!

At that moment Steele became conscious of a need to protect the force from excessive criticism for the inept way in which the affair had been handled. Steele himself had directed the campaign competently from Big Bend; it was his men who had let him down. They had attacked Charcoal's camp without giving him a chance to surrender and had let the Indian slip through their fingers.

In the weeks that followed, the officer made a number of statements about the attack which were simply not true as he attempted to show the force in a good light. First, he maintained that Charcoal had fired the first shot in the battle. In his report to the commissioner he claimed that "when the men were quite close to the tepee the cracking of a dried branch alarmed the fugitive, who was seen as he emerged from the tent, and who fired a shot at Insp. Jarvis, which almost took effect. The murderer fired four more shots from the bush. The Police and Indians fired a volley in return, but were obliged to desist lest they might shoot the squaws and children."[9] Later, for his annual report, he amended the statment to read that Charcoal "fired several shots, one of which almost took effect upon Inspector Jarvis."[10]

Yet the witnesses told a different story. Green Grass, the chief scout, said flatly, "I . . . fired at Charcoal first, knowing perfectly well that Charcoal was armed and prepared to shoot the first man he saw."[11] Similarly, Yellow Bull reported seeing his fellow scout fire the first shot and claimed that he himself had been the next to shoot. At no time did he see the fugitive use his rifle.

"Several Indians gave evidence," commented *The Macleod Gazette*, "as to what took place when Insp. Jarvis' party discovered prisoner in the timber. It is practically the story as it had been told, except that none of them saw or heard Charcoal shoot, and they all swore that the first shot was fired by Green Grass, of Insp. Jarvis' party, followed quickly by shots from all the rest."[12]

Charcoal himself told much the same story. "I heard someone in the brush," he said. "I then heard a gun shot. . . . When I went out of the tent there were lots of guns going off fast. The bullets made the noise they make when they come very close. . . . I did not shoot at all that time."[13]

Yet Major Steele stuck with his story, even with his own scout's statements before him. Eighteen years later, he still claimed that "the cracking of a dried branch alarmed the fugitive, who at once left his tent and fired several shots at them."[14]

If Charcoal had not fired a shot, then who just missed killing Inspector Jarvis? The answer probably is that Green Grass, excited by the sudden turn of events, had caught his officer in the crossfire. Constable Gillespie practically admitted as much when he outlined the events following the snapping of the twig. "Its noise betrayed our presence," he said, "for almost simultaneously, 'bang' went a rifle and off flew the . . . hat. None of us afterwards could agree as to what direction the shot came from."[15] That first shot was from Green Grass's gun.

Steele also played down the fact that Charcoal and his family had escaped on Mounted Police horses, but this was news that couldn't be supressed for long. In his first message, sent to Agent Wilson, the major stated only that "his men had traced Charcoal to Lee's Creek where he had stolen two horses."[16] Before long, however, everyone knew that those missing horses belonged to Steele's men; the *Free Press* observed that the culprit left the scene "riding a police horse."[17]

Interestingly enough, if Charcoal's word can be believed, the whole affair might have ended at the timber limit. Since the killing of Medicine Pipe Stem and the attempted shooting of McNeil, Charcoal had thought he was marked for death. His imperfect understanding of the Queen's law had led him to believe that a killing was inevitably followed by a hanging. There had been no opportunity for anyone to tell him differently nor to explain the vagaries of the white man's law. As he said later, "At the time the first party came up, if they had said they wanted to arrest me, I would have dropped my gun and let them arrest me."[18] Agent Wilson felt the same way. "Had the poor fellow been spoken to at the first when seen at the mountains, things might have been different."[19]

Before the attack, all Jarvis had told his men was that "an attempt was to be made to capture Charcoal alive and at the same time no chances were to be taken, knowing that Charcoal was a desperate man."[20] Only after the battle did Jarvis call out to the fugitive, telling him to surrender, saying that no harm would come to him. But by then it was too late; the unprovoked gunfire had only confirmed Charcoal's belief that he was doomed.

In the end, the "Battle of the Timber Limit" proved to be something of a farce. Charcoal had been attacked without warning, yet he had outwitted and outflanked the police and had done so while accompanied by two unwilling wives and a boy. But Major Steele, the old military strategist, knew that this was only a skirmish; ultimately he would win the war. The might and right of the Queen's justice were on his side, so it could end no other way.

Chapter eleven

After leaving a false trail near the Montana border Charcoal turned his family northward and forded the Belly river not far from the Big Bend detachment where Sam Steele lay sleeping. North across the Cochrane lease the two horses plodded, crossing the Waterton River, and passing west of the Kootenai detachment. They traveled slowly now, for both animals were worn out from two days of patrols and a night of steady travel with double loads.

Charcoal wanted to reach the protective slopes of the Porcupine Hills forty miles away, where the neighboring Peigan Indians had a timber limit. From there, he could get help from his mother, Killed Twice; his brother, Running Crow; and several other relatives who lived on the Peigan Reserve. But at sunrise, when he realized that the police horses were of no further use to him, he made for the tall cottonwoods on the Oldman River. There his wives used the saddle blankets and their few remaining possessions to make a camp while he went out in search of food.

The sun was overhead when Charcoal came to the thick woods at the confluence of Pincher Creek and the Oldman River. This was an ancient camping ground of his people, and as long as he could remember, a white man had always had a house or trading post here. Back in the days before the police, a bearded Long Knife from the south used to sell whiskey at this place, and for years afterwards a man named William Henry Lee had run a cattle ranch. During the past few years, a Frenchman, Mose Legrandeur, had lived here, operating a stopping house for the benefit of travelers on the Macleod-Pincher Creek stagecoach line.

Hungry for food, Charcoal crept close to the house, anxiously watching for signs of danger. He had no way of knowing that the owner had gone that morning to attend Mass in Pincher Creek, leaving his wife and three children at home.

As Charcoal approached the door, gun in hand, one of the youngsters sighted the prowler and told his mother. Rumors and wild stories about Charcoal's rampage had spread throughout the entire ranching area, so as soon as Mrs. Legrandeur saw the armed Indian and his furtive manner, she immediately guessed his identity. Hurriedly she pushed the children into the bedroom closet and huddled with them behind the closed door.

Charcoal knew they were there, but his only interest was food. That morning, Mrs. Legrandeur had finished baking four loaves of bread, and food from the noon meal was still on the table. Setting his rifle near the door, the Indian scooped up the loaves, a chunk of cooked meat, and a butcher knife. Then, leaving as quietly as he had come, he dashed into the trees and was soon out of sight.

When he was gone, the children cried and screamed in fright, begging their mother to get help. Luckily for her, Constable Kerrigan rode up about ten minutes later, on his way to Pincher Creek. After hearing her story, he was about to leave for reinforcements when a Peigan Indian named Joe appeared. Recruiting him as a messenger, Kerrigan sent the Indian on the ten-mile ride to Pincher Creek, while he started to search the wooded river flats.

At first, Insp. A. R. Cuthbert didn't believe the story Peigan Joe told after he galloped up to the detachment. Only a day earlier a message had come from Major Steele saying that Charcoal was afoot and surrounded at the Blood timber limit. It was unlikely he would suddenly show up thirty-five miles away just a few hours later. Yet the tale had to be checked, so he set out for the Legrandeur place, leaving instructions for Constables Maylor and Ambrose to follow as soon as possible. By the time the inspector reached the scene, Kerrigan had already discovered the two winded horses tethered in the brush. After hearing Mrs. Legrandeur's tale and examining the animals, one of which carried the telltale MP brand, Inspector Cuthbert realized that Charcoal was indeed among them.

The officer tried to organize a massive search along the river bottom, but the Peigans had no wish to become possible targets in the policeman's deadly game. Only Peigan Joe and the constables remained to probe the thick willows and cottonwoods. At the same time, Cuthbert sent a messenger scurrying to Macleod with the news of Charcoal's latest raid. There the information was relayed to Major Steele at Big Bend, who berated the bloody inspector for sending the message via Macleod instead of directly. Calling off his intensive manhunt along the boundary line, the major made plans to take a large contingent of policemen and Indian scouts northward on the following morning.

At the Legrandeur ranch, Cuthbert kept up the search until nightfall, then returned the horses to their original location in the faint hope that Charcoal might come back for them. Reinforced by Constables Hatfield and Lewis, he put the two men on the thankless duty of watching the decoys all night.

At headquarters in Macleod, there was great excitment when the news was received of Charcoal's sudden raid. Inspector P. C. Primrose was dispatched to the scene with six men, arriving at Legrandeur's well after midnight. Headquarters also sent messengers to the detachments at the Leavings and Mosquito Creek, warning them to watch for the renegade in case he tried to flee north. As an extra precaution, Corporal Grabill was assigned the duty of riding to the Blackfoot Reserve to tell the staff that Charcoal might come there to hide with friends. Grabill left at eight o'clock in the evening, and by riding steadily all night and changing horses en route, he completed the ninety-four-mile journey in ten hours.

Down on the Blood Reserve, three scouts guarded Charcoal's empty house that night, while another two patrolled the Choking camp, watching the houses of brothers Left Hand, Goose Chief, and Bear Back Bone.

As the evening of 18 October drew to a close, a small army of police and scouts was poised for attack. The Blackfoot Reserve and Leavings and Mosquito Creek detachments were on the alert; Legrandeur's, Charcoal's, and the Choking camp were staked out; and search parties were camped at Bright's ranch, Big Bend, and Macleod, all waiting for the first rays of dawn. In total more than 100 Mounted Police and Indian scouts were on the trail of the elusive offender.

Oblivious to the events taking place around him, Charcoal, now horseless, made camp in the thick brush about three miles downstream from Legrandeur's. He and his family had shared the meat and bread, and when the sun was fading in the western sky, the Indian set out in search of mounts. Leaving the wooded valley he walked south across the flat prairie to a low hill which provided a good view of the whole area. Lying in the grass like some scout from the buffalo days and using the spy glasses he had captured, he spotted two herds of horses grazing about a mile to the west. He was about to approach them when a pair of horses appeared near the edge of the river.

He was being followed!

But no, as the animals came closer he saw they were riderless. One he recognized as a black racehorse belonging to a Peigan named Little Leaf; the other was a blue roan. Curiously he watched them cross a small coulee and approach the first herd of horses. This was not their herd, as they soon discovered, so they moved over to join the second bunch.

After sunset, Charcoal had no trouble roping the black race-horse, and a short time later he was back in camp, the blue roan behind him. The heavy police saddles, of no use with the Indian ponies, were cached in the bushes. Just before setting out, the Indian carefully walked upriver for some distance, through the mud along the shore, then just as carefully walked backwards in the same footprints. Hoping the ruse would throw his pursuers off the track, he took his family to the horses and headed out into the darkness, northwest towards the Peigan timber limit.

Before dawn they had reached the winding course of Tennessee Coulee which led to the thick pine forests on the Porcupine Hills. This high ridge had been a landmark for countless generations; running parallel to the Rocky Mountains it stood like a massive bulwark against the rolling prairies to the east. Thirty miles long from north to south, its bristly, tree-covered slopes gave it the distinctive appearance which caused the Blackfoot to call it *Kai-ska'hp-ohsoyis* — the porcupine tail.

At its southern end, 11½ square miles had been set aside to give the prairie-dwelling Peigans a place to cut logs for houses and corrals. The thick forest also offered shelter from prying eyes, a haven for a hunted man.

Charcoal chose a campsite not far from Tennessee Coulee on a butte close to an outcropping of large, flat rocks. This gave him a vantage point from which he could survey the entire land below. Perched on the hill, he could see where the dry coulee joined the Oldman about ten miles south. Beyond that, nestled out of sight in a valley, was the village of Pincher Creek; farther still was the familiar outline of Chief Mountain.

So much had happened! Only a week had passed since he had tried to find a messenger to go before him to the land of the dead. Red Crow's dogs had repulsed him, the Indian agent had eluded him, and McNeil's spirit had been denied him because of a potted flower. Since then, all he had been able to do was run from the police who wanted to put a rope around his neck, bury his body in the ground, and trap his spirit forever.

If he had done these things thirty years earlier, Charcoal would have been a great warrior. All the Bloods would have praised him for killing a man who had seduced his own relative. Not even Medicine Pipe Stem's brothers could have complained, for they would have been too ashamed. As for shooting a white man, that would have been a brave deed, something to be extolled with pride within the sacred ground of the Sun Dance lodge.

That's how it would have been in his father's time. And in his grandfather's time.

Now everything was different. The white men who ruled their lives said it was wrong to do these things. The police had the guns; they had the rope; they had power. Even to kill a fornicator who broke the unwritten rules of the tribe was now wrong. The Indian laws meant nothing; only the white man's laws counted. When he had violated these, Charcoal knew he would soon die. The white man had said so. Since then they had hunted him, chased him, and shot at him. What further proof did he need?

Looking around, Charcoal surveyed his plight. His family had only the clothes they wore, and each night the air was growing colder. There was no food, no lodge, only two horses, saddle blankets, rope, a butcher knife, and gun. He knew the police would be after him again, so he needed more horses and provisions if he expected to stay free.

That evening he set out with his eleven-year-old stepson for the Peigan Reserve. But he had a problem. Until this time his wives had never tried to escape when he left camp, for Pretty Wolverine Woman had been afraid for her sons. If they had tried to run and been caught, Charcoal would have murdered them all; if she had fled and left the boys behind, they alone would have been killed. Even after the attack at the Blood timber limit, there was still one boy left to discourage any thought of flight.

Charcoal needed the lad to bring back an extra horse, but he could not leave the women unguarded. The only solution was to tie them up until he returned. If he was killed, well, it wouldn't matter.

Riding double with the boy behind him, Charcoal retraced his path of the previous night, a fifteen-mile journey down the grassy slopes to the Peigan Reserve. He had visited there many times in his free days, so the countryside was familiar. Like many Bloods, he was fond of gambling so he knew which Indians owned the best racehorses and where they grazed.

The Peigans were aware that Charcoal was near, and like the Bloods, they were terrified. They too knew how unpredictable a crazy coyote could be. It would fly into the face of danger, kill without reason, sometimes even attack its own body.

As soon as the news of Charcoal's raid on the Legrandeur's was circulated, many men brought their best horses in from the prairie to their corrals or to tethers near their houses. At night, they locked their doors, closed their lodges, and sat in fear. Even in the darkness, Charcoal could sense the change. He avoided the river bottom near Legrandeur's, thinking the police would still be there. Instead, he rode farther downstream near Beaver Creek and the agency, where silent cabins and lodges seemed to sit breathlessly as though waiting for him to pass.

At last he came to the home of New Robe, who owned a good

herd of horses. A few of them were grazing some distance away, but his best riding stock was penned up near his cabin. Boldly Charcoal rode to the corral and was trying to open it when a fearful inquiry came from behind a closed door.

"Don't be afraid of me," Charcoal answered calmly, as he wrestled with poles on the corral.[1] But, disturbed by the knowledge that he had been discovered and finding the corral securely fastened, he mounted his horse and rode off with the boy into the night.

A short time later he came to the home of Tail Feathers Chief, a man the white people called Commodore; his horse was tied to a hay rack close to his cabin. Leaving the boy in the brush near the river, Charcoal guided his horse to the corral, tied it, and crept towards his quarry. The animal moved restlessly as the figure approached out of the darkness, then snorted. Tail Feathers Chief, sleeping fitfully, grabbed his gun and was over to the door in an instant, peering out into the night.

"What are you doing?" he called.[2]

The answer was a rapid shot from a Winchester. As the Peigan ducked back inside, Charcoal dashed to his horse and galloped away. Later, he circled around to pick up the boy, but the lad was gone.

Alone now, Charcoal abandoned any thought of further horse raids and went in search of food and clothing. Making his way along the river, he came to a row of houses belonging to Jack Spear, Big Face Chief, Crow Flag, Cross Chief, and his own brother, Running Crow. As he approached, Charcoal could hear sounds of laughter coming from the cabin of Big Face Chief. Inside, the owner's wife and Mrs. Spear were playing cards on the floor while their husbands talked and the boys slept in the corner. The window was covered by one of the gray blankets issued by the Indian Department; a cosy warmth issued from a big cast-iron stove in the middle of the room, its metal doors open so that the coals rippled and glowed, giving off a shimmering light.

A dog barked. The laughter ceased. Someone said, "Charcoal's coming," and the lamp was extinguished.[3] The noise of trotting hoofs came up to the door; a moment later the rider knocked without dismounting. No one answered; he knocked again.

"I saw the light in your house," said the voice in the night. "Come and open the door."[4]

In a flurry of excitement, those in the house tried to hide. One crouched behind the stove; another climbed under the small table, and one woman, 200 pounds of quivering fear, tried to force her oversized body into a tiny cupboard. In later years, the description of their plight was a source of undisguised merriment in story-

72

telling sessions, but at the time no one was laughing. They knew that Charcoal rode with death.

Braver than the others, Big Face Chief crept to the window, lifting the bottom of the blanket so he could see their midnight visitor. When he recognized Little Leaf's black horse, he had to look no further.

Impatient, Charcoal knocked again. "Where is the house of my brother, Running Crow?"[5] Big Face Chief responded, then sighed in relief as he heard the rider move off to the next cabin. Soon there was a distant tapping, a door opening, and a voice crying "*Oki, oki*, come in!"[6]

Entering his brother's house, Charcoal found they were expecting him. Running Crow had packed a bundle of clothes, a quantity of dried meat, and some bannock which his wife had just cooked. Charcoal ate his first good meal in three days, telling his brother of the events which had made him a hunted man. Now everyone was afraid of him. But it didn't matter, for all he wanted to do was to kill a chief. Now that he was on the Peigan Reserve, he would go in search of their Indian agent, Harry Nash, or their head chief, Crow Eagle; either one would do.

As they were talking, the dogs on the west side of the village began to bark. Quickly Charcoal grabbed the food and clothing, loaded it on his horse, and rode off into the willows and saskatoons which grew in a large grove behind the cabins. At one point his horse almost stumbled into an old cellar, but at the last moment the animal leaped through the air, its forefeet striking solid ground and its hind legs scrambling up the bank. After riding twenty feet into the brush, the fugitive stopped and listened.

Two Mounted Policemen from the Peigan detachment rode casually up to the cabins, the dogs yapping at their feet. Big Face Chief, who was the first to see them, excitedly ran out crying, "Charcoal was here! He just left!"[7] The policemen were fluent in Blackfoot, but neither seemed convinced that the story was true. The entire reserve was edgy; already several supposed leads had proved to be nothing more than rumors or suppositions.

The constables rode once around the grove of willows and saskatoons, not realizing that their prey was standing, deathly still, only a few yards away. They could see nothing in the darkness, but they assured the excited Indians they would organize a search in the morning.

Then unconcernedly, they rode to the last cabin in the line and went inside. Now the Peigans understood; the police had gone to the home of Cross Chief to see his guest, a girl named *Nohka'ki*. She was young and attractive, but thoroughly immoral, moving from man to man and from place to place. She was not related to the Cross Chief family, but they had taken pity on her, letting her stay with them. There had been gossip that one of these police-man — the Peigans called him Little Catcher — had been sleeping with the girl. The two men would be spending the night there.

Charcoal stayed in the trees until he was sure the red coats would not be back, then quietly trotted off towards the hills. First there had been seven in his family, then four, now three. He didn't know what had happened to the boy, but he was sure he would be caught and turned over to the police.

As the net slowly tightened, Charcoal could feel the frustration and fear that gripped him each time he was prevented from attaining his goal. He did not have the arrogant, haughty demeanor that a warrior might have displayed fifty years earlier, when he was truly in command of the plains. Rather, his actions were like those of a desperate, drowning man, grasping frantically as a swirling flood engulfs him. Gone were the buffalo herds, the airy tepees, the days of wandering across endless hills and horizons. At that time a man could look upon his children with pride and hope. He could see his sons become warriors like himself, to carry on the prestige and reputation of his tribe.

Now, after fifteen years of reservation life, what did the average Indian see before him? Some, who were more easily adaptable, saw reason to hope that their sons would become farmers and ranchers, and would use the ways of the white man to find happiness and success. But these were in the minority. All that most Indians saw, if they ever thought about it, was a sha-dowy future in a tribe which would ultimately disappear from the face of the earth. Tuberculosis, scarlet fever, measles, and other diseases were killing off more and more people every year. The Indians were like the buffalo; as each season passed there would be fewer and fewer, and one day there would be none.

And while they lived, it had to be according to the white man's rules. This fact Charcoal had accepted without anger or frustra-tion. It was simply a fact. The Indian agent controlled their rations, so he controlled their lives. The Mounted Policeman controlled their wanderings, so he was both their guard and their guardian. The missionary came with his God, and if this is what gave the white man his power, it must be strong.

A few years earlier, in 1885, some Indians had thought they could stem the tide of the white man's advance. "If we are to be mastered by the whites," they had said, "and to receive only the crumbs from their tables, it is better for us to be killed by bullets than to starve ignominiously."[8] Their solution had been to rise in rebellion, but within weeks the white soldiers had descended upon them like an endless hoard of locusts. The battles had been lost, the chiefs jailed or forced to flee, and the superiority of the white man confirmed forever.

By the 1890s, the new order seemed to have been accepted passively on all reserves. Yet beneath the surface there still simmered frustration and anger; the Indians were like caged animals, ready to explode in rage but aware of the hopelessness of any action. The white man's ways were accepted on the reserves, but often they were merely a thin veneer which covered the traditional culture of an essentially warlike people.

Sensitive observers were alert to this situation. A writer in *The Macleod Gazette* noted that "It is only the presence of large numbers of police in the country which keep the Indians in order. It is absurd to attempt to lull ourselves into the belief that the Indians have become reconciled to the new order of things, or that their feelings towards the whites are any kindlier than they were 25 or more years ago. They remain submissive simply because they have sense enough to know that, in the presence of a large armed force, any other attitude would be disastrous to them."[9]

Their old enemies across the line, the Sioux, had learned that bitter lesson during the 1890s. After years of hard and brutal wars against the American army, the Sioux were finally defeated and placed on reservations. Like their Canadian cousins, they had no love for the white man but had learned that confrontation led unavoidably to death.

The only reason for hope among the Sioux were the visions of a Paiute Indian named Wovoka, a holy man who said that if the Indians followed his teachings, performed the Ghost Dance, and believed in paradise, everything would return to the way it had once been. Wovoka called upon his followers to be industrious, honest, virtuous, and, above all, peaceful.

In 1890, when the Sioux first heard about this new religion, they had sent a delegation to Wyoming to discover more about it. They were told that all the believers would be raised into the air while a new land rolled over the old, sweeping the white man before it. After the holocaust the Indians would be lowered to earth where they would meet their friends from the old days, the land would be filled with buffalo and deer, and sickness and death would disappear.

By the time this "Ghost Dance" religion spread to the Sioux, it had taken on several additional tenets: if a believer danced until he fell into a trance, he could visit the land of the dead to see his relatives; if a man wore a cotton ghost shirt, he was immune to the white man's bullets; and if a feather was placed in a white man's hair, it could render its wearer insane. Thus the peaceful visions of Wovoka took on a more aggressive tone and helped to lead the Sioux back along the only road to freedom that they knew: war.

In the end, the believers were set upon by the American army at Wounded Knee and when it was over, 146 men, women, and children lay dead on the frozen battlefield. Some of them still had remnants of their ghost shirts clinging to their bodies. That was when the Sioux separated their dreams from the cruel realities of life.

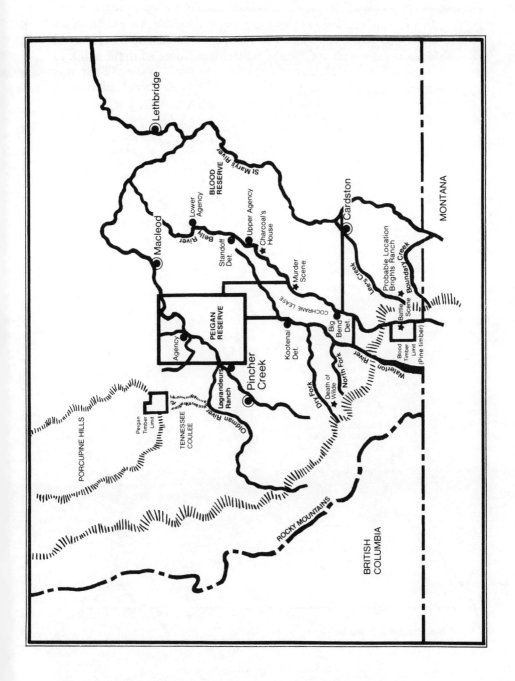

The south-west corner of Alberta was Charcoal's world in 1896.
The reserves and timber limits set aside for the Blood and Peigan
tribes provided refuge to him during his adventurous weeks
of freedom.

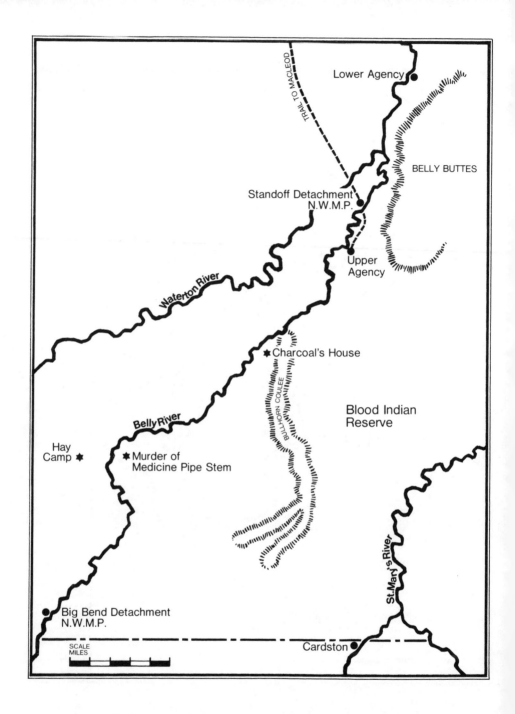

Charcoal's adventures started with a murder on the Blood Reserve and ended there six weeks later when he was betrayed and captured. During his weeks of freedom, the Blood holy man could easily have fled to the United States, but he chose instead to remain within riding distance of his own reserve.

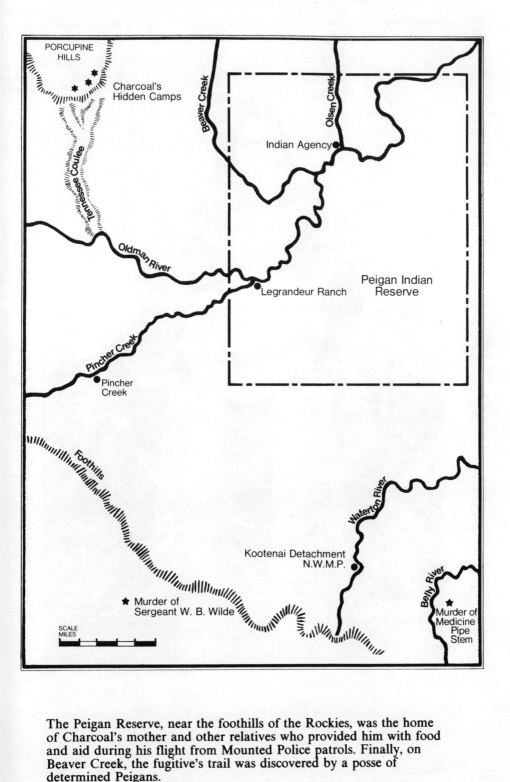

The Peigan Reserve, near the foothills of the Rockies, was the home of Charcoal's mother and other relatives who provided him with food and aid during his flight from Mounted Police patrols. Finally, on Beaver Creek, the fugitive's trail was discovered by a posse of determined Peigans.

Charcoal

Top: The All-Smoke ritual being performed on the Blood Reserve in the 1890s. The man on the left is believed to be Charcoal.

Women at the ration house on the Blood Reserve, 1897

Fire Steel and wife. Although he was a medicine man, Fire Steel took his own son to Charcoal to be cured of an illness.

Pretty Wolverine Woman, wearing her holy woman's headdress, in about 1930.

Medicine Pipe Man Returning With a Crane War Whoop was known to officials as Medicine Pipe Stem. He was killed by Charcoal in 1896.

GLENBOW-ALBERTA INSTITUTE

Yellow Creek, a brother of the murdered Medicine Pipe Stem, was one of those who alerted police to the crime.

Red Crow, head chief of the Bloods, was one of the people Charcoal
considered killing.

James Wilson, Indian agent for the Blood Reserve. When Charcoal failed to kill Red Crow, he chose Wilson as a target.

Top: Headquarters of Indian Agent James Wilson, at the Lower Agency on the Blood Reserve, 1890s.

A camp of tepees on the Blood Reserve

After fleeing from the Blood Reserve, Charcoal took refuge in the timber limit, or Pine Timber. Here he was attacked by the Mounted Police; the ridge over which he escaped can be seen in the background.

At one point Charcoal fled north to the Peigan Reserve. There Crow Eagle, head chief of the Peigans, was one of his potential victims.

When Charcoal made an evening call at the home of Big Face Chief
on the Peigan reserve, he struck terror into the entire household.

Top: Eventually Pretty Wolverine Woman and Sleeping Woman managed to escape from their husband. This large glacial erratic near the Waterton River provided a place they could hide from Charcoal. To the Bloods, it was a holy place.

Cardston, a Mormon town on the southern outskirts of the Blood Reserve, was the object of a hit and run attack by Charcoal after his wives left him. It is seen here in the 1890s.

Goose Chief and wife. He assisted his fugitive brother, Charcoal, and was threatened with imprisonment for doing so. However, no legal actions against him were sustained.

Left Hand, wife and child. In order to save his infant son's life, he agreed to betray his brother to the police.

Major Samuel B. Steele.

Steele in about 1899.

Top: North West Mounted Police headquarters at Macleod, from which point the search for Charcoal was directed by Major Steele.

Blood Indian tepees on the flats near Macleod, 1897. The haphazard arrangement of the camp is in significant contrast to the geometrical order of police headquarters.

Insp. P.C.H. Primrose directed part of the search near the Peigan Reserve.

Included in this group of Mounted Police officers is Insp. A. R. Cuthbert (back row, left), who was criticized by Major Steele for his failure to transmit a vital message with the urgency his superior thought it deserved.

Insp. G. E. Sanders was in charge of the manhunt in the field.

Top: These men at Big Bend detachment assisted in the Charcoal investigations.

Many of the principals involved in the Charcoal manhunt were photographed at Standoff detachment in 1894. Left to right, Interpreter Henry Carmell, Const. Charlie Aspen, unidentified, S. Sgt. Chris Hilliard, unidentified, Colonel Jarvis's sister, Maj. Samuel B. Steele, and Insp. A. M. Jarvis.

Top: The Blood Indian scouts proved to be Charcoal's greatest foes. Seen here at the Standoff detachment are, left to right, Calf Tail, Black Eagle, Big Rib, Many White Horses, Tail Feathers, Many Mules, and Meat Mouth.

Sgt. W. B. Wilde, seated at center, was photographed a year before his death. Seated with him at the Pincher Creek detachment are, left to right, Constable Gould, Scout Holloway, Constable Willis, Constable Ambrose, Constable Bruder, and Constable Hatfield.

Funeral procession for Sgt. W. B. Wilde, who was killed by Charcoal.

Steele's Ibex mine in British Columbia, 1896.

Chapter twelve

On Monday, 19 October, Major Steele set out from Big Bend with his small army of policemen and scouts. There thirty-two in all, sixteen scarlet-coated police and sixteen Indians from the Blood Reserve. A few of the police had heavy jackets, while the scouts wore colorful blanket coats, cartridge belts, and wide-brimmed western hats. All were armed.

Steele led his men along the trail to the Kootenai detachment and due north to Legrandeur's, arriving shortly after noon. He noted that two patrols under Inspectors Cuthbert and Primrose had searched the river bottom, while Indian Agent Harry Nash and a party of Peigans were scouring the area across the river, closer to the agency.

During the day, Primrose had stumbled on Charcoal's old camp where Davidson's two police saddles were discovered. A further search disclosed the moccasin tracks along the river, ending on a gravel bench upstream. This caused a flurry of excitement, with patrols being dispatched to see if the trail appeared farther along. A couple of hours later a Peigan tracker pointed out the telltale marks which showed that Charcoal had doubled back on his own trail.

While this was going on, Inspector Cuthbert first searched the Oldman River all the way to South Fork Pass, then returned to the Legrandeur ranch. He got back just in time to greet Major Steele and receive a withering blast for his tardiness in getting news of the raid to Big Bend. In vain the inspector tried to explain that the only messenger he could find was a young boy who refused to go to Big Bend but agreed to take a dispatch to Macleod. Once there, the message had been forwarded to the major by a police courier — but not quickly enough for Steele.

Cuthbert was angrily ordered back to his detachment at Pincher Creek where he was to ready an outfit for crossing the mountains into British Columbia. There was an outside chance that Charcoal might escape by that route, and a message to Fort Steele would warn the local settlers.

Later, after cooling down, the major reasoned that an officer was not needed for such a mission. Instead two constables and a scout were assigned the thankless task. But for the rest of the manhunt, the discredited Cuthbert was denied any real responsibility. "At no time during the search," he stated regretfully to Steele, "were there more than 3 or 4 men under my immediate orders, and these were chiefly employed in carrying dispatches to yourself and officers in charge of the searching parties."[1]

The Fort Steele couriers took with them Steele's summary of the search to date. "I have been after him for ten days," said the major, "assisted by four officers and 100 police and Indians and have been rummaging the plains, swamps, and mountains for him. Several of the men and officers have been fired on and have had 'close calls'."[2] He said that Charcoal was "short, 5'8 or 9, stooped shoulders, 40 years of age, very much wrinkled, bow legged, and sometimes has a bad complexion. He has a squaw with him who is an accomplice, rather good looking and a good size and another squaw of his who is medium sized and *not* good looking. However, the man is the one of the most importance. He is a desperate man and has given us the days of the hardest riding done in the force."[3]

By this time, the frustration was beginning to show. More than 100 men were scouring the country for a lone bow-legged Indian in an advanced stage of tuberculosis. Not only had he outwitted the patrols, but inept officers and delayed messages had plagued the campaign from the beginning.

Questions were being asked about the efficiency of the force, with the Winnipeg *Daily Tribune* commenting that "the pursuit has now been going on a week, and the capture seems no nearer than ever."[4] *The Macleod Gazette,* run by an ex-policeman, felt it necessary to rise their defense. "Major Steele and the officers and men under him," said the editor, "deserve the greatest credit for the energy and perseverance with which they have followed this Indian. They have kept him dodging, and are giving him a very uncomfortable time of it."[5]

Perhaps some men would have been grateful to have a defender; Steele was not. He wanted results, not excuses, and the failure to capture Charcoal reflected on the entire force. Worse, if the Indians believed they could get away with murder and defy the police, all the years of bringing law and order to the West could be threatened. Rumors to this affect even reached the press during the manhunt, one paper commenting, "It is said that a number of other Indians have become affected by Charcoal's success and have made threats against the Police."[6]

Steele shared this concern. "We have been firm with the Bloods for a long time past," he commented later, "and I believe that they like and respect us, as much as they can any whites. To retain this respect and obedience we must be firm."[7]

The yardsticks used by Major Sam Steele to measure his wards were simple ones. The good and progressive Indians were separated from the shiftless and lazy ones on the basis of their acceptance of the white man's dress and his work ethic. When Steele assumed command of the Macleod district in 1888, the Bloods were not civilized enough to suit him. "The young bucks were always ready for war," he observed, and "although well fed they would turn out at night and raid the ranches for cattle and horses."[8]

But even worse was the persistence of the Sun Dance, that annual ritual which enabled the Bloods to reaffirm their faith in the sun spirit. "When I took over command of the Macleod district," recalled Steele, "the Sun Dance . . . kept the red man from becoming civilized, and the mischief was enhanced by the practice of the older men of 'counting their coups,' i.e. relating to the assembled warriors their real or imaginary feats of valour in war. This conduct encouraged the rising and recently initiated braves to commit crimes, such as horse and cattle stealing and raids upon their hereditary enemies, the American Indians."[9]

Steele's goals were simple. With the co-operation of the Indian agent and with or without the help of the chiefs, he would stamp out the Sun Dance, prohibit the Indians from owning guns, and severely restrict their movements off the reserve. The promise made at the Blackfoot treaty giving Indians free access to wander through the Queen's domain was proving impractical. If they were ever going to progress, they would need to stay at home where they could look after their gardens and livestock, and receive regular visits from the missionaries.

During his ten years as Mounted Police commander in the district, Steele had worked hard to bring about these changes. "I am strongly of the opinion that the time has come for disarming the Indian," he had told his commissioner in 1891.[10] Even though the police had succeeded in pursuading the Indian Department to prohibit the sale of ammunition to Indians, this attempt had failed. The United States border was only a few miles away, and in Montana there was a plentiful supply of cartridges for their Winchesters, Sharps, and other guns from the buffalo days.

Although complete prohibition against guns was never introduced, Steele continued to press for the seizure of the Indians' weapons. By 1896, by fair means or foul, the campaign appeared to be succeeding, for in the Blood tribe of 1,700 persons, there were only thirty-seven rifles, eight shotguns, and eight revolvers.

Of these, Charcoal was the owner of a Winchester rifle, as were his brothers Goose Chief and Bear Back Bone.[11]

Where the Sun Dance was concerned, Major Steele encouraged the Indian agent to put on a sports day at the same time in the futile hope that this would draw the young people away from the sacred ritual. When this didn't work, he decided to play down the ceremony's impact upon the tribe. "From personal observation and careful inquiry," he told his commissioner in 1893, "I am convinced that the festival has almost entirely ceased to have any significance, except perhaps to the old people . . . and many of the Indians themselves did not attend."[12]

Keeping the Indians on their reserves was another problem. At one time Major Steele put forth a proposition which to him was utterly simple and workable, allowing the police to arrest an Indian at any time or any place, with or without a warrant. "They were wards," he reasoned, "and we were officers of the Crown, therefore there was no chance of a miscarriage of justice."[13] This astounding statement sounded more like Steele's law than the Queen's law, and even though he felt he had official support, Steele's contention was finally overruled by a local judge.

But the major persisted in his efforts. When the Indian Department introduced a system whereby the Indians needed passes to leave their reserves, he was quick to enforce it. On one occasion when two Blood chiefs led a small group of parents off the reserve to visit their children at a boarding school, Steele sent out a patrol to intercept them. The entire party was arrested, held in the guardhouse for a day, and then herded back to the Blood Reserve.

When the suggestion was made that the pass system violated the intent of the treaty, Steele was horrified and gave examples of wandering Indians who pillaged empty ranches. "If Indians will act in such a manner when they know that they are not permitted to roam about," he commented, "the result, should they think that the police have not the power to order them to return to their respective reservations . . . may be better imagined than described."[14]

In time, Steele's efforts were effective. He saw the instances of cattle killing decline as Indians found it harder and harder to leave their reserves. There were fewer complaints from ranchers, and each year saw the Blood Indians more tightly penned within the borders of their reserve. In fact, when Steele had married Marie Harwood of Quebec in 1890, he had not hesitated in bringing her to his headquarters in Macleod, and by 1893, the major could hazard a yawn as he wrote to his commissioner that "during the past season everything has gone on with almost monotonous regularity."[15] There had been only 190 criminal cases in the district

107

during the entire year, most of them minor and many committed by white men. It had seemed as though the frontier period of Indian trouble was behind him.

But now there was this Charcoal business! On Tuesday morning, 20 October, the major learned about the abortive raid during which Charcoal had opened fire on Commodore. Within the hour, Steele had the search parties in the field and was on his way to headquarters to get more reinforcements, arms, and ammunition.

As if he didn't have enough problems, the major's mining interests also urgently needed his attention. He had learned of an opportunity to buy the Florence mine, with a possibility that the Black Diamond claim might also become available. In each case, a new company would have to be incorporated.

Moreover, the development of his Ibex properties was proceeding apace. While he was away, Steele's mining secretary had been putting the finishing touches to the Ibex company so that stock could be offered for sale. The decision was made to have a capitalization of $300,000 raised through the sale of twenty-five cent shares. Initially 200,000 shares would be put on the market in Macleod, Vancouver, Winnipeg, and Toronto. A few would even be sent to London.

The claim had been acquired early in September, and by October the trails had been cut, cabins built, and work started on a cross-cut tunnel to tap the main silver vein at a depth of about 100 feet. It sounded very promising, but the work needed the major's constant attention; instead of that, he was chasing a damned Indian all over the prairies.

Upon arrival at Macleod, Steele sent Insp. G. E. Sanders out with six men and even pressed his veterinarian into service, giving him four men to help search the Peigan Reserve. On the chance that Charcoal might move northward along the Porcupine Hills, the major summoned Sgt. Maj. F. W. Spicer, ordering him to take six Indian scouts on a five-day expedition along the eastern slope of the hills.

While in Macleod, Major Steele telegraphed reports of the latest incidents to the commissioner, at the same time asking for belated permission to hire as many Indian scouts as he needed at the rate of fifty cents a day. This was approved by return wire, but his request to offer a $200 reward for the killer was met with cold, stony silence.

Meanwhile, Inspectors Primrose and Jarvis had gone to Commodore's cabin to investigate the shooting. When they arrived, Big Face Chief was on hand to tell them about Charcoal's nocturnal visit to the row of cabins. This time his story was believed and a search instituted in the nearby brush along the river. Later in the morning reinforcements arrived with one patrol under Inspector Cuthbert and a party of civilians under rancher John Herron.

Just as the search was getting underway, word came that Charcoal's boy had been captured! According to the story, his stepfather had hidden him in the bushes, warning him not to run away. A few minutes later, he had heard a rifle shot and, afraid that he might be killed, he had scampered off blindly into the valley. Later he came to the cabin of a Peigan named Wood Man, where he had spent the rest of the night; next morning he was delivered to the Indian agency.

The boy was obviously as frightened of the police as he was of Charcoal, but after a great deal of urging, he agreed to show them his stepfather's camp. In order to conceal their approach, two Blood scouts in ordinary dress accompanied him, with Sergeant Camies and a small patrol of police and Indians following at a short distance. Behind them, another force under Inspectors Cuthbert and Sanders brought up the rear.

The boy led them to Tennessee Coulee, and by nightfall the searchers were staring down at the dead fire in Charcoal's abandoned camp. A trail into the hills was followed for a short distance, but the tracks soon disappeared. He had eluded them again!

The party camped on the slope of the hills that night and continued the search next morning. It was, as Inspector Sanders observed, a frustrating experience.

"One of the many difficulties we had to contend with," he said, "was single Indians and white men getting scared and running from us, causing a lot of waste of time in their pursuit and taking a great deal out of our horses.

"Whilst in the Porcupines we had several of these wild-goose hunts. On this occasion we had one of them after a white man, which I will describe in order to illustrate how easily they happened. An Indian scout who was in the hills about 4 miles to the right of my party saw a man riding in the distance; he went towards him, and the man started to gallop off. The Indian signalled and we started in pursuit right through the Porcupine Hills. The scout being in the lead, all the pursued person saw was an Indian topping each divide after he had passed it. The pursuit extended for 15 miles when we found the pursued to be a cowboy who thought Charcoal was after him."[16]

When Major Steele returned to the Peigan Reserve to direct the manhunt, he ordered a search of Running Crow's house. The shortage of clothing in the place and information from the neighbors indicated that the man was helping Charcoal, so Steele had him taken into custody. At the same time, the police were instructed to pick up any other relatives of Charcoal on the reserve in case they might "render him further assistance."[17]

No charges were laid, and none of the Peigans was ever brought to trial, for there were no grounds. Steele's law had taken over again.

Chapter thirteen

Stretched flat on the bare rock, Charcoal had seen the hunters approaching. They looked ridiculous; two scouts with the boy trying to act innocent while the rest of their army followed behind. With his spy glasses, the fugitive could see every detail, even the fear on his stepson's face.

Charcoal didn't smile at the silly parade approaching his hill. There was little to smile about these days. The constant running and hiding had left him so weak that at times he could hardly move. The pains in his chest were with him constantly, while sharp hunger pangs reminded him of his desperate plight.

Perhaps he shouldn't have threatened to kill the Peigan Indian agent or the head chief. Both men would be on the alert now, expecting him with every strange hoof beat and with every dog that yapped suddenly in the night. Either man would have been a good spirit messenger; if he had killed them, he could have finished the whole business, his faithless wife, then himself.

The trio was getting closer now; the boy was leading them on a straight path. Rising slowly, Charcoal returned to his wives and said quietly, "My son is guiding the police to where we are camped."[1] There was not much to pack, so in a few minutes he took the women and horses deeper into the timber until their trail became obscured in the brush. Tying his frightened wives to trees, he circled around on foot until he came to a number of flat rocks east of his original camp. There he stretched out again to brazenly watch them approach.

The riders were less than a quarter of a mile away when Charcoal dropped behind a rock, letting the two scouts and boy pass within a few yards of him. Then, before the main party arrived, he slipped back into the trees.

Oh, coyotes are crazy,
They catch what they want,
Hai ya, hai ya, ho.

Even though he was sick, hungry, and frightened, Charcoal knew he had taken the coyote role and believed he had to live up to it. That was part of his power. Perhaps the Bear Knife was gone, but there were other spirit helpers who could protect him, tell him what to do.

A long time ago, animals and men had been able to talk to each other. The animals could foretell the future, warning their human friends of danger. The coyote was one of the wisest of these animals, having been a friend of *Napi* the trickster at the time the world was born. Now the coyote avoided man, no longer speaking to him, but he was daring and cunning, knowing when to fight and when to run and hide. When a coyote went crazy, frothing at the mouth, he was one of the most fearsome creatures on the prairies. Still wise, he cared nothing for his own life, stealing food from the camp dogs, attacking a man without warning, shooting his fine hairs into an Indian's body.

Charcoal remembered hearing about an old Peigan named *Minipoka* who was attacked by a crazy coyote. The man was looking for his horses, his rawhide lariat dragging behind him through the snow, when he felt something tugging on it. Turning he saw a large coyote chewing on the end of the rope. He tried to scare the animal away, but it only trotted off to a nearby hill where it howled four times. Before long it was joined by a whole pack of coyotes who circled *Minipoka*, closing in on him.

Another Indian rode by just as the old man was fighting them off; they had not bitten him but he lay lifeless in the snow. The rider took him back to camp, but the medicine man said that the coyotes had shot him so full of their evil hairs that no one could save him.

When a man decided to give up his life, he too could become a crazy coyote; this was the pathway that Charcoal had chosen. Now he was feared by the Bloods and Peigans for they knew that he could kill without reason.

That night, while the police camped on the slopes of the Porcupine Hills, Charcoal rode back to the Peigan Reserve, stopping at a friend's house on the north slope. There he learned that Running Crow and his other relatives had been arrested. He could still expect help from his relative Gray Woman, a wife of Big Bull, who hadn't been picked up. Furry Man, Wolf Tail, and Sunday were others who would not turn away their old friend, in spite of their fears. But it was not the same. A man could always count on his brothers to help, no matter how serious the trouble; there was always a danger that a friend might betray him.

The solution was to go back to the Blood Reserve. He had not seen Left Hand and the others since the trouble had started, yet he

112

had no doubt they would help him. After all, they were his brothers.

Later, two horses with three riders made their way through the darkness of the October night, down from the hills across the river, south past the Peigan Reserve to the Cochrane lease. Before morning, Charcoal had found a secluded campsite on the upper reaches of Dry Fork, a twisting coulee which ended at the Waterton River. From there he was only fifteen miles from Sleeps on Top's cowshed, where the adventure had all started just three weeks earlier. That fatal day seemed like a lifetime away — Charcoal's lifetime.

Now, back within striking distance of the Blood Reserve, he might yet be able to make his mark upon a chief. If not, he would kill one of the red coats; not just one of the ordinary Catchers who patrolled the reserve but one of their chiefs, the ones with yellow stripes on their arms or gold braid on their shoulders. Perhaps he might be lucky enough to meet their head chief, *Spi'tow*, the one they called Steele.[2]

On the next night, 22 October, Charcoal returned to the Blood Reserve. He suspected that scouts would be waiting for him, but by keeping to the thick brush on the river bottom, he could pass within ten feet of a man in the darkness without being heard or seen. In the days on the trail Charcoal's senses had sharpened until they were like those of a warrior in a hostile land. He traveled silently, the black horse moving swiftly in the darkness, never betraying their presence with a snort or whinny.

The Indian scouts were there, five of them, but they didn't see Charcoal come or go. He traveled the last few miles on foot, creeping along paths which he had known for years. His log cabin on the brow of the hill lay dark and deserted, stripped of all its contents by the Indian agent a few days earlier. A short distance downstream, Charcoal quietly let Goose Chief know he was there, entering his house when he received a sign.

It was good to be back.

The family was all at home, his twenty-six-year-old brother, wives Tailfeathers Woman and Funny Blanket, a baby daughter, and their young son, Sacred Dagger. Goose Chief told him all that had happened — the seizure of his furniture and belongings, the constant presence of guards, and the state of fear which existed throughout the reserve. Practically all the outlying ranches and cabins had been abandoned, and fall haying had come to a standstill as people clustered together in large tepee camps at the two agency offices.

Charcoal in turn related his adventures, his escape in the mountains, the black racehorse, the arrest of Running Crow. He reaffirmed his intention of killing a chief — or all of them if he

113

could. But his gun was not working properly; the old Winchester was unreliable. Could Goose Chief part with his?

Regretfully, the brother explained that he had pawned it but would redeem it as soon as he could and gladly turn it over to his warring brother. After all, the Choking band looked after its own, in spite of the hostility and fear on the reserve.

After he left his brother's house, Charcoal prowled through the brush, easily eluding the guards as he made his way toward Bullhorn Coulee. Once there, he found a small herd of Black Eagle's horses grazing on the hillside. Slipping the rope hobbles off the best three, he was soon trotting over the dark prairie, back to his refuge in the hills. It was daylight before he had finished his sixty-mile round trip, but no one challenged him as he rode across the low hills that led to the tree-clad slopes.

With three horses, Charcoal no longer needed to tie up his wives every time he went in search of food. The next night, Pretty Wolverine Woman and Sleeping Woman were with him as he killed a three-year-old heifer. Expertly they skinned the carcass, butchered it, and ate the raw kidney before returning to camp with the meat and hide.

During this time Major Steele and his men continued to scour the hills and valleys near the Peigan Reserve. After the boy had taken the police to the Porcupine Hills on 20 October, the major had blanketed the area with patrols. Sanders and Cuthbert had searched the south end of the hills, Spicer and his Bloods the east. Primrose, Jarvis, and Nash's Peigans had beaten the brush for the umpteenth time along the river while Davidson, damn his hide, was down at Big Bend.

There was no reason to stay around any longer, so Major Steele rode back to Macleod. All he had accomplished was the arrest of Running Crow and Charcoal's other Peigan relatives and the fruitless interrogation of the boy. Back at his office, he found some explicit inquiries from the commissioner, as well as a pile of newspapers dealing with the Charcoal manhunt. "More Murders Near Macleod" bellowed the Winnipeg *Daily Tribune*.[3] "Indian Eludes Pursuers, Riding Away on a Policeman's Horse — Not Caught Yet" laughed the *Free Press*.[4] Even the local Macleod paper was ablaze with the headline "The Murderer Still at Large."[5]

The newspapers were sympathetic, but there was no doubt that settlers for miles around were frightened. The ranchers near Pincher Creek had been warned to guard their stock, and many people who usually left their doors wide open were now locking them at night.

Although there had been no direct criticism leveled against Major Steele or the Mounted Police for the way the search was being conducted, many of the papers were naturally making the most of the story's sensational aspects. Concerned that people in the East misunderstand, C. E. D. Wood, the ex-policeman editor of *The Macleod Gazette*, explained the difficulties.

"Surprise has been expressed that one Indian should have been able to elude all the police and Indians who have been looking for him for a week past," he said. "If these persons knew the country, there would be no occasion for surprise. In the first place the fugitive is a very clever Indian, and in the second place, as long as he is able to remain in the brush or timber, it is next to impossible to corner him.

"A number of the police who are after him are old and successful hands at this sort of business, and they have been assisted by Indians, who should know something about it, and civilians. The brush in the bottoms near the Peigan reserve is so thick that it is next to impossible to force a way through it, and one could pass within a few feet of a man and not see him. Everything that experience and skill can suggest has been done, and we believe that the murderer's capture is only a matter of a very short time now."[6]

Steele sighed. He hoped it was true.

In the days that followed, the false rumors came one after another. First, a Peigan boy said he had seen Charcoal riding along Olsen's Coulee, just north of the reserve, and had been warned away. It wasn't true. Then a Blood named Old Shoe reported seeing Charcoal riding a white horse. Upon investigation it turned out to be a Cochrane Ranch cowboy. Next an employee of the Walrond Ranch, north of Macleod, said that Charcoal's brother, Red Horse, was going to assist the fugitive. This, too, proved false. A short time later, Inspector Davidson reported that three of Black Eagle's horses were missing, but no one could be sure if they had strayed or been stolen. After that, Scout James O'Keefe thought he saw the fugitive north of Bullhorn Coulee, heading towards the ration house, but he couldn't be sure. As Inspector Sanders later stated, "We kept up patrols night and day, receiving information from Indians and others continually, which was investigated until proved incorrect; we also suffered from want of interpreters, as I was unable to supply all parties with some one who understood the Blackfoot language."[7]

The first break had come on 24 October, when Steele received word that Charcoal had been seen driving three horses west across the Cochrane lease the previous morning. That fitted Davidson's account of three horses disappearing from Black Eagle's camp! But it was, as he recorded later, "30 miles south of the Peigan Reserve and 40 miles south of where he was last known to be."[8]

A dispatch was sent to Inspector Sanders, in charge of the

search at the Peigan Reserve, ordering him to call off the hunt and to take all available men to the Cochrane Ranch. Primrose was left behind with five men to keep an eye on the Peigans. Setting out in the evening darkness with his large force of policemen and scouts, Sanders reached the Kootenai detachment at two o'clock in the morning. There he learned that the remains of a butchered heifer had been found near the mountains, about twenty miles up the Dry Fork. Splitting his party, Sanders sent Jarvis south to the Cochrane Ranch while he took the others west to the Hatfield ranch.

The sun was already high in the autumn sky when the policemen reached the cattle-killing scene. The Blood Indian scouts said the heifer had been slaughtered only a day before; its ears bore Hatfield's brand marks. After searching through the brush Scout Green Grass picked up the trail of the three unshod ponies leading westward to the heavily forested slopes at the base of the Rocky Mountains.

Later in the afternoon, the trackers met a settler who informed them that his son had seen an Indian cooking meat farther up Dry Fork on the previous day. Heartened, Inspector Sanders pushed his men along the trail until darkness halted their search.

Now that they were on a fresh track, Sanders sent word back to the others. Jarvis hurried over from the Cochrane Ranch while two civilians, John Herron and G. J. Jonas, came down from Pincher Creek. Farther south, Inspector Davidson posted patrols to prevent Charcoal from escaping south or west across the mountains. Guards were placed at South Kootenay Pass, Belly River Pass, and at key positions along the border. The rest of the men searched Belly River all the way from the Cochrane Ranch to Red Crow's camp.

When Major Steele learned that his men were on the trail of Charcoal, he sent an urgent request to Agent Wilson for another four Blood scouts. It wasn't the fifty cents a day, but a combination of fear and a thirst for adventure which brought forth a further group of volunteers. Throughout the entire search, Major Steele had no difficulty in finding Bloods to help. "After about a week of hard work," said the major, "the Indians would become tired out, fatigued from want of sleep, their clothes torn, moccasins worn out, and horses used up; it would then become necessary to relieve them; they would turn in their arms and ammunition, which would be reissued to those who had been selected to replace them."[9]

As the trail was now on the slopes of the Rocky Mountains, Steele dispatched four pack ponies loaded with ropes and other gear in case Sanders needed them. Then, should the fugitive get across the mountains, he ordered Constables Hatfield and Wilson through the Crowsnest Pass to Fort Steele, to apprise local authorities of the latest happenings and to elicit their aid.

The noose was closing on Charcoal. Patrols waited on the south; the mountains blocked the west. The Pincher Creek detachment was patrolling Castle River and the Crowsnest Pass to the north, while Sanders's trackers were following Charcoal's trail up Dry Fork from the east. For the moment this left an area ten miles square in which the fugitive could roam, but as each day passed his range grew smaller and smaller as the police kept up the relentless search.

On the morning of the twenty-sixth, Inspector Sanders's patrol followed the trail farther west, almost to the head of Dry Fork. From there they turned south over a wooded ridge to the North Fork of Waterton River. By this time, the small Indian ponies were playing out; one by one the Bloods dropped behind until there was only one tracker left. Yet the fugitive's trail was clear enough to the remaining scout that he had no trouble leading the police through the thick pine forests, upland pastures, and heavy underbrush. Towering beside them, only a mile or two west, were the craggy peaks of the Rocky Mountains.

During the night, the fortunes of the pursuers plummeted — leaden skies were finally signaling the approaching of winter. For weeks, the prairies had enjoyed mild weather, but on the morning of 27 October, a thin carpet of snow blanketed the land. For days, the searchers had been hoping for snow so that they could more easily pick up the culprit's trail. But just as the white carpet would reveal new footprints, so did it cover the old.

The trackers were out all day and during the search, a patrol met a hunting party of Stony Indians who reported having seen Charcoal's camp in the mountains. It turned out to be close to the main searching party under Inspectors Sanders and Jarvis, but when the police reached it, Charcoal and his wives were gone. Not until late that night did the searchers again pick up his trail, this time heading due south towards Waterton Lakes. There was speculation that he might be heading back towards the Blood timber limit. If so, Davidson's patrols would be waiting for him.

Major Steele heard each new dispatch with increasing optimism. The cordon had already tightened since the trail had first been sighted, and now the presence of snow had become a decided asset. "I warned Davidson and cautioned him to keep a sharp lookout as the trail had been struck," said the major, "and there was no chance of Charcoal's getting back without eluding large parties under Inspectors Sanders, Cuthbert, Jarvis and Mr. Herron."[10]

Early the following morning, Charcoal raided the outbuildings of a rancher named Cyr, stealing a ham, some chickens, and a blanket. Sanders didn't hear about it until late in the afternoon, but the news threw the search into complete disarray. The Cyr ranch was at least eight miles *due east* of their search area, well out of the mountainous ridges and back on the edge of the prairies.

Charcoal had broken out of the trap!

Sanders was disgusted when he reached the ranch. There was no doubt that Charcoal had been there several hours earlier. "We got no word of it till late in the afternoon," he complained, "although Cyr knew where I was. Had we found out earlier, we would have had a beautiful trail in the snow, but as it was we found nothing but moccasin tracks inside the fence, the snow outside being tracked all over with hundreds of cattle and horses."[11]

Even with a small army of police, Indian scouts, and civilians surrounding the area, Charcoal had managed to slip through the cordon with his two wives. Not only that, but he had disappeared without a trace.

That made five getaways for Charcoal and five defeats for the police. The Indian had anticipated their arrival at his cabin, escaped from the ambush at the timber limit, stolen two police horses at Bright's ranch, eluded a search party in the Porcupine Hills, and now slipped out of the net near the Dry Fork. All this had been done by a sick, middle-aged Indian who was dragging two reluctant women along. His pursuers outnumbered him a hundred to one. They had worn out their horses and replaced their tired trackers, yet after almost three weeks Charcoal was still a free man.

If the Queen's law didn't produce results soon, then Steele's law would have to take over.

Chapter Fourteen

Charcoal had paused only briefly after escaping from the police. His camp was now in a thick grove of trees back on the Dry Fork, he having simply circled around from the head of the coulee to its mouth, leaving the police stranded and confused twenty miles away.

He was lucky to have seen the police a couple of days earlier, or he might never have known that they were on his trail. But those scarlet uniforms could be seen for miles, especially with the help of the officer's stolen field glasses. Once he knew the police were behind them, Charcoal led them south until it looked as though he was heading back to the timber limit, then practiced the old Blood strategy of doubling back. Only this time he hadn't backtracked on the fresh trail but had circled around to the route he had taken a week earlier.

The pace had been a rapid one. The food was almost gone again, the horses were used up, and his wives tired. They still prepared his meals, made camp, and did the other chores expected of a wife; they also shared his food, his problems, and his bed in their mountain camps. Yet they were his prisoners; he knew it and they knew it. If he had killed a spirit messenger, Pretty Wolverine Woman would have been dead by now, perhaps Sleeping Woman as well. In the meantime, they did as they were told, acted like wives, but were afraid to run in case they were caught. This way, if the Mounted Police found Charcoal first, they might live. But they knew that if they tried to escape and were caught they would surely die.

At night they still shared his blanket. A man at war needs the companionship of a warm body; that was why so many men had taken their women on long raids during the buffalo days. It was not good for a warrior to be without a woman for too long. And Charcoal was at war with everyone around him. The Bloods and Peigans wanted to kill him because they were afraid of him. The police wanted to capture him because he had broken their laws.

No. Perhaps they didn't want to capture him; they had opened fire on him at the timber limit without even giving him a chance to surrender. The Mounted Police must be afraid of him, preferring to kill him with bullets rather than waiting to hang him. It was the same with all the others, the ranchers, the settlers, the Indian Department men — they were afraid of him, too.

Charcoal's only allies were his family and the spirit powers. He could rely on Goose Chief, Left Hand, and Bear Back Bone whenever he needed food, and during the passing weeks he found increasing strength in his spirit helpers. These strange voices with no bodies were a part of nature which he discovered during his flight. Charcoal had not realized how much he had taken on the white man's ways while he had been on the reserve. He had been living in a white man's house, eating flour and drinking tea, wearing white man's clothes, cutting hay and tending cattle, and even learning things from the white man's thick book, his Bible.

During those years he had followed the old religion, but he had not been close to nature, not like his forefathers had been. Now, after weeks of sleeping in the open, listening for sounds of danger, watching for his enemies, he was learning the old ways. The crows and magpies told him when strangers were near, the soaring swallows warned him of changes in the weather, the animals showed him their trails through the brush.

Although hungry, tired, and sick, Charcoal was strengthened by the knowledge that nature was his friend. The streams gave him water, the trees sheltered him, the rocks hid his trail. And a special spirit helper guided him, talked to him, and told him how to escape from his enemy. Charcoal's helper was called *A'i-eekina*, a voice which he could hear but couldn't see.[1] Usually it came to him at night, as though in a vision; it taught him a song which would bring him good luck and give him the strength and courage to outwit the police.

Charcoal knew that the Bloods would begin receiving their annual treaty money on this day, 29 October, and that they would be racing horses, making trips to Macleod, and joining together in all-night gambling sessions. Even the chiefs.

Leaving his wives securely bound, Charcoal quit his camp on Dry Fork after nightfall, riding one horse and driving the other two before him. They were worn out and of no further use to him, so he would abandon them where they could easily be found and returned to their owners. That is what he had done with Little Leaf's two horses, the black and the blue roan, a week earlier. Back across the Waterton River Charcoal traveled, ignoring the trail he left in the snow and huddled low in the saddle to ward off the cold. No new snow had fallen for hours, so his tracks crisscrossed countless others during the fifteen-mile ride to the reserve. Boldly approaching the river from the west, he tied the three horses to a tree opposite the reserve, then quietly made his way to the Choking camp. Again he easily eluded the scouts guarding the village, and a short time later he was resting comfortably in Left Hand's house.

After days of camping near the mountains, it was good to relax in a warm house with plenty of beef and bannock to eat. One by one, his brothers came around to see him. Goose Chief, true to his word, produced the .44-caliber Winchester which he had retrieved from Bentley's trading store, together with more ammunition for his brother's cartridge belt. They told him how everyone else would be going to Macleod the next day, but the Choking clan would travel south to the Mormon town of Cardston. They were being shunned by their neighbors, even spat upon by people who suspected them of helping their crazy brother.

After taking a small supply of food and his new rifle, Charcoal made his way to the main Blood camp at the Upper Agency. Tepees were pitched along the entire river bottom as people gathered together for mutual protection from the night marauder. Hardened by weeks of travel, senses sharpened by constant vigilance, Charcoal was a different man from the inept raider who had tried to steal Tail Feathers Chief's horse on the Peigan Reserve. Now, with the cunning and stealth of a coyote, he crept into the center of the camp, not even waking the nervous dogs a few yards away.

At last he found what he was looking for.

Among the sixty tepees pitched closely together in the flat, he had picked out the distinctive painted design on the one belonging to Bull Plume, a wealthy horse owner. Everyone knew about Bull Plume's champion racehorse, a beautiful animal, cream colored and 15.2 hands high. The next day, the owner planned to take it to Macleod for a matched race against the best the Peigans could offer. Several times during the evening, Bull Plume had gone outside to look at it, check its hobbles, and make sure it was safe.

Charcoal found the cream; it was picketed just outside its owner's lodge within sight of a dozen other tepees. The Indian drifted soundlessly up to it, reassured the beast, slipped off its hobbles, and led it away to the nearby trail. Moments later he was astride the animal, galloping off towards his secret lair.

Two decades earlier, to have committed such a deed would have marked him as a true warrior. Entering a crowded enemy camp, choosing the best horse, and stealing it from under its owner's very nose was an act of bravery and heroism. No dog barked; no horse stirred; no one heard a moccasin step in the snow. He had come, taken his prize, and gone.

121

But this was 1896; the days of warfare were but a dim memory. Charcoal was not a warrior but a crazy renegade who had broken the white man's law. His actions were no signal for acclaim but a reason for fear.

Next morning, the Bloods told Agent Wilson what had happened. "The three head of horses said to have been stolen the previous Friday were found on the bench opposite Left Hand's village," he reported in turn, "with saddles and ropes on and the horses in a very much exhausted condition. . . . They had every appearance of having had a lot of hard riding and the saddle marks were still fresh upon two of them while the third showed signs of only having been ridden with a blanket. One horse was very lame and the other two had fresh sores upon their backs while all three had a starved look."[2]

While Charcoal was visiting the Bloods that night, another kind of activity was taking place at his hidden camp. When he had left, Charcoal had tied up the women as usual. This time, however, he had secured them to the same tree branch, Pretty Wolverine Woman with her hands behind her, Sleeping Woman with hers in front. After struggling for some time, the younger wife managed to loosen her ropes enough so that she could lean forward to catch them in her teeth. Then began the long slow process of chewing. And chewing. And chewing.

Finally a cord broke, followed by another and another until at last the rope came apart. Sleeping Woman was free!

Pretty Wolverine Woman had watched the sequence of events in fascination, but her hopes turned to terror when she realized that Sleeping Woman intended to leave her behind. Charcoal had made it clear that Pretty Wolverine Woman had been the cause of their flight; if it had not been for her unfaithfulness, Sleeping Woman would not have been dragged through the fears and hardships of the previous weeks.

As the eighteen-year-old girl prepared to leave the camp, Pretty Wolverine Woman begged to be released. She related how many times she had danced with the Holy Women and how her powers still might be needed if Sleeping Woman expected to get back to the Blood Reserve alive. Hesitating, the younger wife recognized the truth of her statements. Charcoal could easily find his way on horseback in the dark, but they were in unfamiliar country and afoot. Relenting, she cut the older woman loose and together they hurried along the coulee toward the reserve.

They had crossed the Waterton River and were following it downstream when they heard Charcoal in the darkness. Riding his cream racehorse, he was singing his war song as he trotted along the trail near the river. Frantically the women looked around them. They were in a broad river bottom that was bare of trees.

The moon overhead, the glistening snow, gave enough light to reveal every bush and boulder in the valley. Near the river's edge, in a small backwater, they saw an old beaver lodge. Quickly they ran to it, desperately pulled away some of the branches, and cowered against its muddy sides.

Quietly the older woman prayed. She remembered the tale about the man who had been befriended by beavers when lost on the prairie. A terrible blizzard had been sweeping toward him when a beaver had popped its head up from the water and called to him. The Indian had jumped into the river, just as the women had done, and was taken to the underwater entrance to the lodge. Once inside, he was warm and dry. The beavers had looked after him all winter, feeding him the bark of trees and dried berries. They had taught him the beaver songs and ceremonies which he had taken back to his people in the spring.

Now the beaver lodge was the hiding place of Pretty Wolverine Woman and Sleeping Woman, not from a blizzard, but from a different kind of raging storm which could kill them. The high-pitched falsetto strain of the war song came closer, passed by, then faded into the distance.

When Charcoal was gone, the women dashed to the trail, knowing that their husband would soon reach the camp. An hour later they heard his voice again; it was not singing, but crying and wailing like a tormented demon.

"I've been saving Pretty Wolverine Woman," he called out to his younger wife. "She's the only one I really want to kill."[3]

Again the women were far from the protective cover of the trees, but Pretty Wolverine Woman knew they were near a holy place. Quickly she led the girl across the prairie until they came to a huge rock, a house-like mass left there by receding glaciers eons ago. The Blackfoot, lacking knowledge of geological science, had given it a supernatural origin.

Back in the days before man, the only ones on the prairies were animals and a diety called *Napi*. Like man, he was a mixture of wisdom and stupidity, good and evil, stinginess and generosity.

One day, while walking with his friend Kit Fox, he had been bothered by the weight of his robe, for the weather was hot and there was no protection from the sun. In a fit of generosity or laziness, he had spread the robe over a large rock, saying he was giving it away as a present. A short time later when it started to rain, *Napi* missed the robe and sent Kit Fox back to get it. Three times the rock refused to give it up, until at last *Napi* went back himself and snatched it away.

Later, as they were walking along, *Napi* and Kit Fox heard a great rumble. Looking behind them, they saw the rock rolling along to crush them. Kit Fox fled, but the rock was after *Napi;* no matter how much the trickster pleaded, the rock came closer and closer. None of the birds or animals would help him, until at last a flock of night birds came to his rescue. Each time they swooped down and defecated, a large chunk of stone broke loose, until the rock was completely shattered. Its boulders, massive in size, were spread across the prairies from Waterton Lakes to the Bow River, each becoming a holy place and a source of spiritual power.

When the two women reached the rock, the older wife prayed aloud and circled it once, just as she would have circled the holy women's society lodge at the Sun Dance. Then, finding cracks and fissures in its side for handholds, they climbed to the top and lay there trembling.

Soon their husband came riding by, still crying and calling to them. He passed close to the rock, then continued northeast along the course of the Waterton River. Charcoal suspected the women would not be able to find their way at night, so he surmised that they would follow the river down to its mouth, where they would find Day Chief's camp.

Instead, the women waited until he was gone and then traveled due east along the Belly River, passing within three miles of Charcoal's deserted cabin. By sunrise, they had crossed the river and were deep in the trees along its banks. Later, when they came to a number of cabins belonging to members of the Fish Eaters band, they ran up to them looking for protection but found they were locked. The occupants had gone to the Upper Agency for treaty payments.

Continuing along the valley, the distraught women kept a constant watch behind them to see if Charcoal was on their trial. By mid-morning they were still in the brush, away from all the trails, when they heard the sound of a wagon. Excitedly they fought their way through the tangles just in time to see Rides at the Door and his wife disappearing along the trail. Yelling and waving, they caught the man's attention and soon were safely in his wagon on their way to his house.

They learned that just about everybody upriver had gone to the matched races at Crop Eared Wolf's place, not far from the agency. Rides at the Door had stayed at home because of an injured hip and had been on his way for firewood when the women had appeared.

A boy was sent to the races to let the chiefs know the women had escaped. Arriving there he yelled, "Charcoal's women are up at Rides at the Door's place!"[4] In their excitement everybody left the races; in wagons and on horseback they rushed up the river to see the two runaway women. Later, Bull Horn loaded the pair into a wagon and took them to the Mounted Police detachment, everyone following along in a gigantic, festive parade. After weeks of fear and wild rumors, the tension on the Blood Reserve had reached a peak which seemed to burst when the women were found. There was laughter; people chatted and gossiped; everyone thought that Charcoal himself would soon be caught.

For Major Steele the news was good and bad. He was pleased that Charcoal's wives had escaped, but now there could be no doubt that the Indian had broken through the net. Calling off the mountain hunt, Steele moved the search headquarters to the Blood Reserve, bringing Inspector Sanders in from the Dry Fork, Primrose down from Macleod, and Davidson up from Big Bend. The first to arrive was Inspector Primrose, who reached Red Crow's village in the early evening, after losing his way while looking for the camp. With neither scout nor interpreter in his patrol, the inspector could not communicate with the Indians. He thought they said Charcoal was hiding in a house nearby, but when he broke into it, the place was empty. Then he was made to understand that Charcoal would be coming there later that night so, with a group of helpful Indians, he set up a stakeout. Long after midnight, his native friends heard some activity downstream and were off to investigate. Disgusted, Primrose followed them out of the camp but they had disappeared into the night. They'd probably gone home to bed, he concluded, leaving him to bumble around in the dark. At this point, still not understanding what had happened or why he was there, Primrose called off the whole midnight exercise and returned to Standoff.

Inspector Davidson's invasion of the Blood Reserve was more orderly, but no more successful. Starting from Big Bend, his patrol spread out across the valley of the Belly River, traveling downstream. Every clump of trees, every thick matting of brush was searched as they made their way to Red Crow's village. In the meantime, all but ten of the Indian scouts on the Peigan Reserve had been discharged as the search moved onto the Bloods' land. The remaining Peigans were instructed to circle the snow-covered hills surrounding their reserve, looking for signs of nocturnal visitors.

On the Blood Reserve, Charcoal's two wives were relieved to be home. Both had suffered from exposure and a lack of food, but were in surprisingly good health. The sheer terror of their ordeal had kept them going while they prayed for deliverance from the man who had once been their loving husband. Sleeping Woman was particularly resentful about her treatment, blaming the older wife for causing the incident. Pretty Wolverine Woman, on the other hand, was at last freed from her nightmare experience which each day had been taking her closer to certain death. Yet she would never speak to people about the ordeal, preferring to surround herself with the comforts of her religion. She did, however, co-operate with the police and before she was placed in protective custody in Macleod, she provided them with a detailed description of their last campsite. A patrol of sixteen men led by Scout Eagle Child and ex-racehorse owner Bull Plume, went to the Dry Fork, but so well hidden was the camp that they were unable to find it. In any case, they knew the fugitive would be miles away by now.

As Major Steele juggled his troops, he realized he was no closer to catching Charcoal than he had been two weeks earlier. If anything, he was farther from his goal, for now the Indian was alone, traveling easily and quickly from place to place. It was only a matter of time before he would either kill again or run to the United States where they could not follow.

In his flight, Charcoal was compounding his crimes. In the beginning, he had killed his wife's lover, obviously finding him in a compromising position. If the villain had only given himself up then, no court in Canada would have hanged him. But no, he had to go out and show everybody what a great chief he was by trying to kill a white man. Yet even on that charge a good lawyer could have gotten him off lightly, for McNeil was already back on the job. Since then, the Indian had added two or three thefts to his list, besides shooting at the Peigan Indian, Commodore.

What did the blighter want, anyway? The Indians kept saying he was crazy; maybe they were right. But he didn't act like an insane man, not the way he covered his trail, eluded the patrols, and moved his camps. He was a very smart customer, but worse, he was making the Mounted Police look foolish.

To this point, Major Steele had gone by the book. He'd sent out patrols, hired Indian scouts, followed every lead and every rumor. Nothing. Now it was time for Steele's law to take over.

An Indian boy, Round Nose, had gossiped about Charcoal's visit to the Blood village during the night; this, combined with the finding of the worn-out horses across the river, made it obvious to the police that Left Hand and the other brothers were helping Charcoal. There was no direct proof, but the time had come to cut off the fugitive's source of food and supplies. Concurring in this strategy, Major Steele and Agent Wilson determined to round up the entire family, including its intractible leader, Left Hand.

Under these orders, S. Sgt. Chris Hilliard was sent out to the Choking camp where he found only one brother, Bear Back Bone, still at home. Though he was ailing, in an advanced stage of tuberculosis and with less than a year to live, the man, his wife, and two-year-old child were all taken into custody. His oldest boy, Crane Chief, was already in jail where he had been languishing for three months awaiting trial on a cattle-killing charge.

The rest of the clan had gone south to Cardston where they

126

planned to spend their treaty money, camp for a few days, and pick up some supplies for Charcoal. He would visit them there to get the tobacco, tea, and other essentials for a man on the run.

As soon as the police learned where the family had gone, Staff Sergeant Hilliard, with Farmer Clarke, an interpreter, and a constable, set out after them. The next day the entire Indian group was placed under arrest — men, women, and children. There were Left Hand, his wives Otter Woman and Different Cutter, and their tiny baby, Baldface Pinto Rider, a sickly child carried in a blanket on his mother's back. Then there were Goose Chief, with his two wives and their children, one of whom was a girl, Telling a Dream, only a few weeks old; Knife and his family; Crane Chief's young wife, Traveling About; and Left Hand's aged mother, Longtime Buffalo Stone Woman.

By the time he had brought them together, Hilliard had twenty-three people in custody, nineteen of them women and children. Left Hand, as leader of the family, was separated from the others and sent north under escort in the late afternoon, traveling all night and reaching the Standoff detachment at sunrise. The remainder, horses, travois, dogs, women and children, followed at a more leisurely pace, arriving at the outpost at sunset. From there, the clan was taken to Macleod where they joined Bear Back Bone and his family in the guardhouse.

Although Major Steele later reported that he had arrested Bear Back Bone "for aiding and abetting the fugitive,"[5] and Left Hand "with twenty-two other relatives, consisting of squaws and children, for assisting the Indian," no charges appear to have been laid.[6] The only person ever charged was Goose Chief, who was accused of supplying Charcoal with the Winchester rifle, and even this was later dismissed.

So Steele's law was in effect. Twenty-six people were locked in the Macleod guardhouse, with no charges being preferred against them. Such youngsters as five-year-old Sacred Dagger and one-year-old Singing Kit Fox were apparently considered by the major to be a threat to the security of the community.

With winter in the offing, snow covering the ground, all help cut off, and patrols scouring the area, the end of the manhunt was in sight. In a matter of days, Charcoal should be cornered and brought to earth. Yet Steele couldn't help admiring his adversary. He was, the major observed, "a Blood Indian whose pluck and endurance were a wonderful example of what the greatest of natural soldiers is capable of, when put to the test."[7]

Chapter fifteen

Charcoal was alone.

Surrounded only by the spirits of his supernatural world, he moved through the snow-covered countryside, silent as the owl in flight, wise as the coyote on the trail, determined as the gray wolf following a buffalo herd. His fear was tempered with the knowledge that he had his ghostly advisers to help him, voices to counsel him so he would not fall into the white man's trap before his work was done.

Now that he was by himself, Charcoal was both exhilarated and afraid. Severing the last cord with the real world left him entirely in the company of those whom he believed gave him his power. He was stronger than he had ever been, even though his body was thin and emaciated. He was a warrior who could creep into an enemy camp, taunt his pursuers, outwit all adversaries. He was nothing like the sickly, mild man who had been cutting hay for the white man a few weeks earlier. He was a real man, *nita'pikwan*.

Yet he was worried that Pretty Wolverine Woman was no longer with him. At the time of killing the boy, Charcoal had vowed that he and his wife would die together. She was to blame for everything so she had to die, but not until he had killed his spirit helper and sent him on his way to the land of the dead. Even now, Pretty Wolverine Woman was probably back with her mother, laughing at him, just as she and her lover had laughed at him before. When the time came to die, he hoped he would have no trouble finding her.

All night he had looked for the two women along the Waterton River until, at sunrise, he stood on a hill overlooking Day Chief's camp. No one was stirring, so he knew he had missed them; they must have crossed over to the Belly River and gone to the Upper Agency.

After hiding near the river all day, 30 October, Charcoal reverted to his original plan, the one which had been interrupted by the flight of his wives. He knew the Bloods and Peigans were congregated at Macleod after receiving their treaty money and that some of their chiefs would be among them. Macleod, too, was the home of Steele, *Spi'tow*, the chief of all the Mounted Police who were following him. If he were lucky, Charcoal might find a chief to kill; whether white, Blood, or Peigan, it didn't matter. Even if a white man's body was buried in the ground he could still be a messenger, for the missionaries had explained that a Christian's spirit left his body at the moment of death, never to return.

Arriving at Macleod after nightfall, he saw that the Bloods and Peigans were camped on the river bottom west of the Mounted Police barracks. Hiding the cream-colored racehorse in the trees, he walked boldly along the trail, the cloth hood of his Hudson's Bay blanket coat pulled over his head to leave his face in shadows.

Although it was after sunset, the camp was alive with activity: people visited, gambled, and joined the night singers as they serenaded each tepee. Charcoal proceeded among the people unnoticed, until he came to a small crowd standing in front of an open lodge. A hand game was in progress inside, the two teams lined up so that everyone could be seen. Charcoal looked for a chief; there was none. Over to one side he saw a stranger whose hairstyle showed him to be a Kootenay Indian. For a moment the fugitive fingered his rifle, toying with the idea of killing someone from a tribe which the Bloods had once considered to be their enemy. But no, he was not a chief.

Later that night, when most of the camp was asleep, the outlaw approached a tepee where Hind Bull and some other Bloods were playing stud poker. Someone heard the footstep outside and jokingly said to the other players, "I'll bet that's Charcoal."[1]

Joining the fun, Hind Bull took a bucket and stuck it out the flap, saying, "Hey, Charcoal! Go get some water at the broken ice. We'll make some tea and give you some."[2] Much to his surprise, a hand in the darkness took the pail; a few minutes later, the water was placed inside. Still laughing, Hind Bull made the tea, held a cup out the door, saying, "Brother, here's the tea for you."[3] It was taken, drunk, and the empty cup passed in.

It was a great joke. Not until later did they learn that their nocturnal servant actually had been the feared killer, demonstrating his calmness and humor in the midst of danger.

Charcoal's daring visit had produced no chiefs nor Mounted Police officers. Before daylight, he had slipped away again, riding south across fifteen miles of prairie to the Blood Reserve, and by dawn he was safely in the trees across from the Fish Eaters' camp. During the day, a few people passed close to him, but none of them was Red Crow or any of the other chiefs. On one occasion a patrol started to search along the river bottom, but he galloped easily away, following the narrow twisting trails until he was far upstream.

For two days he stayed close to Red Crow's village, watching for the chief during the day, prowling through the camp near his house at night. Charcoal knew that his brothers had gone south so, on the second night, he sought his old friend Fire Steel, the medicine man whose boy he had once doctored and saved. As he approached the top of the coulee where his friend lived, the dogs rushed out, barking and snarling in his direction. The night was a moonless black, yet the snow reflected enough light to let Charcoal see a figure leave the cabin and walk to the rim of the gully. Looking blankly into the darkness, the man spoke; it was Fire Steel.

"Charcoal!" he called out. "If I was here alone I'd invite you in for tea, a smoke, and something to eat. But I've got two people here now, and one of them is Meat Mouth; you know him, the police scout. He has a gun. If it wasn't for that, I'd ask you in."[4]

Standing there, not knowing whether there was anyone else in the darkness or whether Charcoal was looking for a person to kill, the old medicine man continued.

"I came out to give you a warning, Charcoal," he said. "When you go to any of the camps looking for horses, don't go near the corrals. The people have put their unbroken animals in the corrals so that they'll start moving around and making a noise if you come near them. If you want a fresh horse, don't go near the corrals."[5]

Charcoal was grateful for the advice, but he was still tired and hungry as he watched Fire Steel return to his cabin. Believing that his brothers would have food and shelter for him in Cardston, he decided to set out for the tiny village, twenty-five miles south. Following Bull Horn Coulee, close to the route he had taken when he first fled from the reserve, he reached the protective banks of Lee's Creek just as the sun was edging over the horizon.

Well hidden and far from the search parties, Charcoal slept fitfully all day, alert for any suspicious sounds as he rested from his two days and nights of vigil at Red Crow's. In the evening, he rode to the outskirts of Cardston where the Bloods usually camped when trading in town. There he was surprised to see none of his brothers' tepees. Where were the familiar designs of Left Hand's buffalo-stone lodge or those of Bear Back Bone, Goose Chief, and Knife? Creeping over to the camp, he caught a startled old woman collecting firewood; she babbled a few words about the entire family being arrested, then fled in terror to her lodge.

Charcoal was furious.

This trouble was his doing, not theirs. The police had no right to put his brothers, nieces, and nephews in iron cages. They wanted Charcoal, not women and children. Until this time, he had not seriously looked for a white man to kill, not since he had shot at Farmer McNeil. Tonight was different; it was a time to become as crazy as the coyote whose habits he imitated. Just as he had gone openly into an Indian camp looking for a chief, so would he now go to the Mounted Police, looking for a man with stripes on his sleeve.

Quietly, Charcoal made his way to the Lee's Creek detachment, where Inspector Davidson, Cpl. William Armer, and Constable Bushe had just returned from a patrol. Stretching out full length on the ground, Charcoal rested his Winchester on the top of a watering trough, the barrel pointed towards the men's quarters across the square. In the darkness, he heard someone walk to the stable and return, but there was no chance for a shot. A few minutes later, the door opened again; this time he saw a policeman with two stripes on his sleeve walk towards a shed behind the house, carrying a lantern with him. From there, he started across the square to the stables.

Charcoal could see only the glowing light, but assuming it to be held waist high, he waited until it was thirty feet from him, then fired slightly to its right. The cry of surprise, rather than pain, told Charcoal that he had missed. Without waiting to take a second shot, he scampered to his feet, recovered his horse, and dashed off westward across the prairie.

Cursing his bad luck, Charcoal, hungry as ever, but angry now and heedless of danger, stopped at the first convenient ranch, about three miles from town, broke into a storehouse and took enough bread, butter, fat, and flour to last him for several days. Knowing that the area would soon be swarming with police, he laid a false trail and turned his racehorse northward, hoping to reach Macleod, forty miles away, long before dawn.

Bull Plume's horse, which had served him so well, had now reached its limit. Although a hardy animal, it could not maintain the pace required by a man on the run, and by the time they reached the Belly River, the horse was worn out. Regretfully, Charcoal abandoned the beautiful beast, picking up a runty pony which was grazing loose near the Blood camps. It was slow and stupid, but it got him to the tepees outside Macleod before sunrise. There he turned the animal loose, picked up two fine racehorses, a sorrel and a brown, which were tethered near their owner's lodge, took a saddle as well, and with the first rays of the sun he was deep in the brush along the Oldman River, feeding on the rancher's stores and looking admiringly at his two latest acquisitions.

The night had been a long and remarkable one. Although tired and hungry, Charcoal had visited the Indian camp at Cardston, fired on Corporal Armer at Lee's Creek detachment, pillaged a rancher's storehouse, stolen an Indian pony at Belly River, abandoned it, and taken two racehorses and a saddle at Macleod. All in less than twelve hours.

Yet he had not succeeded in his primary mission: to kill a chief or police officer to take the message of his forthcoming arrival in the spirit world. Not until then, only then, could he end the task of throwing his life away.

Word of the shooting at Lee's Creek, as usual, caught Major Steele by surprise. For the past few days, rumors had been flying out of the Blood Reserve about Charcoal being seen near Red Crow's village. There was even one story around that he had gone to the Cypress Hills, and another that he was across the line in Montana. The last account had sufficient merit for Steele to notify the American Indian agent to be on the lookout for him.

Instead, the fugitive had now turned up at Cardston, where he had tried to ambush a Mounted Policeman!

"About 7:45 P.M.," Corporal Armer wrote in his report, "I went to the stable, watered and fed the horses, but could not find any oats, as during my temporary absence from the Detachment the key of the oat bin had been mislaid. I returned to the house to ask Constable Bushe if he had seen the key. We both looked for it and failed to find it. I then went to the lean to on the west side of the dwelling house to see if any oats were left in sacks.

"I then went towards the stable carrying the lantern only. I had it in my right hand. To get from the stable to the house it is necessary to pass close to the well and watering trough. While walking towards the trough and about thirteen paces from it, I saw a flash and a report, and felt a bullet pass between my left side and arm.

"I immediately rushed back to the house and found Constable Bushe getting his carbine. I got mine. I instructed Bushe to go round by the back of the house and I went to the place from where the shot was fired; neither of us saw anyone."[6]

The bullet had gone through Armer's left sleeve, causing a slight, grazing wound between the elbow and shoulder, and going out through the back of the shirt. At the time of the shooting, the corporal had been holding the lantern to his right, away from his body; had it been closer, the bullet would have gone through his heart.

A search of the parade square turned up moccasin tracks and a piece of rawhide line. When recovered, the bullet proved to be from a Winchester .44.

Inspector Davidson immediately notified the search co-ordinator, Inspector Sanders, who was still working out of the Upper

Agency on the Blood Reserve. At three o'clock in the morning, patrols under Sanders and Primrose arrived at the Mormon settlement, ready to start the search at daybreak.

Meanwhile, a courier sent to Macleod arrived at dawn, almost paralleling Charcoal's journey along the same route. Major Steele was stunned. Alone and without help, Charcoal should have been on his knees by now, begging for mercy. Instead, he had attacked a Mounted Police detachment and could easily have killed one of the NCO's. As the day wore on, Steele got further reports of the search.

"A Mrs. Lamb reported," Steele later wrote, "that during the night, after she had gone to bed, her husband being away from home, she heard someone gallop furiously along the trail, which was close to her house. She knew from the rate at which the person travelled that it was not her husband and she was very much frightened. She then heard a noise in the storeroom which was built behind the house, as if some person had entered, and was pulling things about. On entering the storeroom the next morning she saw that a quantity of bread, butter and flour had been stolen during the night."[7]

Near the house, Scout Green Grass had picked up the trail of an unshod horse and followed it up Lee's Creek for two miles, where it crossed a trail leading to the Layton ranch. At one point it had looked as though Charcoal were heading west for the timber limit, but suddenly the hoofmarks had disappeared. Only later had they discovered that the Indian had shrewdly doubled back on his path at a point where his trail couldn't be traced.

The next report to reach Major Steele came from the Blood Reserve. The cream-colored racehorse had been found standing in a coulee on the Black ranch, about a mile north of the Indian agency.

"He had a very sore back," said Agent Wilson, "giving unmistakable signs he must have had a considerable amount of hard riding without a saddle, and his knee and hips were scratched as if he had been ridden hard through brush. The horse was tired out and did not offer to move when approached."[8]

During the day, a third piece of news hit the shaken major. Two Peigan racehorses had been stolen from the Indian camp within a mile of his own headquarters! Not only that, but the thief had taken a saddle which had been leaning against its owner's tepee.

On the off chance that Charcoal had gone back to the Blood Reserve, Major Steele hired a number of Indians, issuing them with rifles and ordering them to search the Belly River. He also organized a flying patrol, consisting of a non-commissioned officer, two constables, and two scouts. Outfitted with pack horses, they were ordered to keep on the move, following up every lead, rushing to the place where Charcoal had last been seen. Operating without daily orders from headquarters, they were to move rapidly to the scene of a sighting, pick up the outlaw's trail, and stay on it until Charcoal was captured.

Damn! Damn! Damn! Charcoal had been on the run for three weeks, and the police were no farther ahead than they had been on 14 October. The newspapers seemed to have given up on the police, which was a mixed blessing; the weekly *Macleod Gazette* had not even mentioned the manhunt in their last issue. What could they have said? Charcoal had been on the Blood Reserve, but the police had missed him? Charcoal had shot and wounded a corporal, but the police hadn't seen him? Charcoal had stolen two horses from the Indian camp beside the Mounted Police headquarters, but the police hadn't even heard about it until the next day?

At last, the Indian agent came forward with a suggestion. He wanted to put pressure on Charcoal's brothers — or were they his half-brothers? — so that they would surrender him. The agent was sure that the Left Hand family had its price, and if the police could find it out what it was, Charcoal might fall into their trap. Major Steele had some misgivings about the plan. It sounded too much like Cain and Abel, brother against brother; more important, he doubted whether it would work. But he was desperate, for all the rumors, tips, and search parties were producing nothing.

The price of Left Hand's and Bear Back Bone's co-operation was easy to determine. Since they had been confined to jail, the condition of Left Hand's sick baby had worsened; the Indian was afraid the boy would die if kept in confinement, and daily he begged to have the mother and child released. That was his price.

Bear Back Bone, on the other hand, was worried about his eldest son, Crane Chief. The young man had been in jail for three months facing charges of cattle killing. The confession of an accomplice was certain to convict him as leader of the ring, and he could look forward to two or three years in the Stony Mountain Penitentiary. In 1896, an Indian boy sent to jail for any length of time usually died of tuberculosis due to the close confinement. Two or three years for Crane Chief was the same as a death sentence. The release of his son was Bear Back Bone's price.

With Major Steele's concurrence, Agent Wilson saw the father of the sick baby first. "I had a long talk with Left Hand," reported Wilson, "pointing out to him that he and his three brothers and their families were all in prison for harbouring and assisting Charcoal and that by so doing they had committed an offence and were liable to be punished; that the chances were they would all be

134

kept in prison till Charcoal was arrested, even supposing that took months; that I did not like to see them prisoners; that I was friendly with him and had always done a good deal for him and his family in the way of giving them wagons, harness, cattle, work, etc., and that now I called on him to come to my assistance."[9]

Like a spider weaving a web around its victim, Agent Wilson laid out the problem, then presented his simple solution. "I told him that I would see his wife and he were liberated, provided he would do his utmost to get his brother. I also pointed out that some of the party in confinement were sick and that it would be to all their interests to see Charcoal arrested. He was asked to proceed to his own house and stay there, to keep his house lit, windows uncovered so that Charcoal could see he was back on the Reserve. . . . I explained to him that if Charcoal came to his house he was to persuade him to give himself up for the sake of his relatives, promising that I would see he got a fair trial, but that if he refused he must try and arrest him."[10]

When Agent Wilson was finished with Left Hand, Major Steele took over. "I told Left Hand that if he did not [co-operate] he would be very severely punished for aiding and abetting the fugitive and that his mother, wife and relatives, who were in the Guard Room, would have to stand their trial. I impressed this upon him so deeply that I felt certain that he would do his utmost."[11]

Left Hand, anxious about his baby, agreed to co-operate with the police. According to Wilson's report, he shook the agent's hand and said that "If I would only allow him out with his wife and sick son, he would do all I asked him."[12] On 5 November, Left Hand, wife, and child were released from the guardhouse.

Next, Major Steele interviewed Bear Back Bone. He informed the Indian that his boy was due to appear in court on 12 November; if the father went out and captured Charcoal before that date, Steele "would not press the matter of cattle killing against his son Crane Chief."[13] It was a deal the old man could hardly refuse, the life of his son. The price was high, but so were the stakes.

Steele's law was now in command. Two men, who had been held for six days without charges, were now released with their families — one to get his sick infant son out of jail, the other to free the guilty leader of a cattle-killing ring. In exchange, Left Hand and Bear Back Bone were expected to perform only one duty. To betray their brother.

Over the years the Choking band had been noted for its family squabbles, its wild and spoiled ways. Charcoal had always been the odd man out, the half brother who was not related to the wealthy side of the family. Yet in spite of family differences, they had always seemed to unite against a common enemy.

They had all taken an interest in native religion, with Charcoal, Left Hand, and Bear Back Bone all joining the Horn Society at the same time. The three had often participated in ceremonies together. One winter, early in 1893, the brothers had gone with other holy men to help White Buffalo Chief celebrate the finding of his missing horses. A blizzard had blown through the reserve, scattering his herd, leaving the young stock in danger of freezing to death. In desperation, White Buffalo Chief had prayed that if the horses were found, he would sponsor an All Smoke ceremony. When the horses were located, Charcoal, Bear Back Bone, Left Hand, and ten others were invited to his house to sing their holy songs all night.

The three brothers had an impressive list of religious affiliations, holy objects, and songs. Among them they belonged to the Horn Society, Crazy Dog Society, Crow Carriers Society, Parted Hair Society, and Black Soldiers Society; they had songs to go with their painted tepee designs; they owned medicine pipes, fringed war shirts, sacred belts and headdresses, and, of course, Charcoal's fearsome Bear Knife.

The family, no matter how much they bickered, was a close one. This, in itself, had often cut them off from their neighbors, bringing them together as they argued, fought, got into trouble, and created general unrest in the camps.

Now the white man had given them a choice, the health of a baby and the freedom of a boy in exchange for a coyote-crazy brother. There could be only one decision.

Chapter sixteen

While the police were searching Lee's Creek and the Blood Reserve on 3 November, Charcoal followed the snowy path to the Peigan Reserve, going from there to the Porcupine Hills. This time he chose a campsite a few miles east of his old location, just in case the Peigans were still patrolling the area.

The scouts, not the Mounted Police, were the ones who were giving him all the trouble. They could read his signs, discover his strategy, predict his movements. By themselves, the police would have been helpless; the pursuers he had to fear were his own people. Green Grass, Yellow Bull, Tail Feathers, Bob Tail Chief, Red Crane, Weasel Bull, Bear's Smoke, and the other scouts knew the country almost as well as Charcoal. They were familiar with the trails, the camping places, and the people to whom the fugitive could turn for help. Persistent and untiring, they patrolled the Blood Reserve, the Cochrane lease, and into the foothills, looking for the crazy one who might kill them all.

As a medicine-pipe owner, Charcoal had the songs and prayers which he believed enabled him to control the weather. As he drew closer and closer to the spirit world, he found comfort in this knowledge, faithfully performing the rituals each day. In his mind, there was no doubt that his prayers were being heard, for the weather had remained unseasonably mild, even into November. There had been only a couple of inches of snow, and much of it had blown into the coulees and river valleys, leaving the benchlands and hills almost bare.

When Charcoal rode down to the reserve the next night, his friends on the north slope passed on the good news that his brother, Running Crow, was back home. He had been held by the police until 26 October, when the search had shifted south to the Dry Fork. Charcoal realized that his brother's house was probably being watched, but he could still slip into the village to visit him. His mother, Killed Twice, was back in her cabin as well.

137

During the next three or four days, Charcoal rested in the Porcupine Hills, sleeping near the places where the spirits dwelled — high lonely buttes, vision-quest hills, and burial places. At one camp he took the throat strap from a halter to tie the tops of some low trees together to make a shelter. In another place, his bower of branches was on the crest of the hill.

From there, Charcoal could look for miles out over the land. To the west the rugged line of the Rocky Mountains was silhouetted against the gray November sky. Southward, stretching before him, the rippling prairies undulated like snow-clad waves dashing against the massive base of Chief Mountain. Eastward, the rolling hills broke their rhythmic pattern to become a flat and barren plain.

From where he stood, the land within his gaze looked like a separate corner of the world. His corner. A place where he was born and a place where he soon would die. Down there, armed with guns, the scouts and police were looking for him, to shoot him or to put a rope around his neck.

Idly, the Indian shifted his rifle, cradling it in his arms. This gun, after all the days of running, hiding, and starving, was now his only link with the real world. His children had deserted him, his wives had flown, Left Hand and the others were in jail. He was alone on the frozen slopes of the Porcupine Hills, alone with his horses, his gun, his spirits.

Yet his body was real; it craved food, warmth, and the other needs of man. Even his namesake, the coyote, could not creep through the brush nor taunt his enemies without the comforts of food, a den, and a mate. A crazy coyote wasn't that crazy.

Catching his horse, Charcoal rode out in the early evening, back to the Peigan Reserve. He was standing quietly in the trees, not far from Running Crow's house, when he saw a woman come out of the farthest cabin and go down by the river. She was Cross Chief's youngest wife, an attractive girl barely out of her teens. Silently the fugitive followed her as she walked along, breaking dead branches off trees to be gathered for firewood on her way back.

Charcoal hummed to himself as the girl wandered deeper into the brush.

Oh, coyotes are crazy,
They catch what they want.
Hai ya, hai ya, ho!

When she was close to the ice-choked river, the Indian suddenly stepped behind her, clasping a hand over her mouth. In terror she recognized the lean, pock-marked face, saw the broad butcher knife in his hand, the rifle on the ground. Weeping,

138

almost blubbering in fear, she submitted as he pushed her to the snowy ground. He raped her there, wordlessly, within a few hundred yards of the house; then, like a gray prairie wolf, he was gone.

Sobbing, clutching her blanket to her body, the girl stumbled home to tell her husband what had happened. Cross Chief's first impulse was to go to the police, but he changed his mind. What good would it do? The last time Charcoal had been to their village, the police had come, not to look for the wanted man, but to sleep with his young house guest. The news would only bring shame to the family and not help the police to catch the crazy one.

The next day the gray clouds released their long awaited burden of snow over the foothills and prairies. Swirling and plunging and drifting, it piled deep in the coulees, settling like a cold blanket over the entire countryside. That night, when the skies cleared, the temperature plummeted to thirty below zero.

Charcoal's tragic adventure had started with a sexual embrace in the lonely cowshed; was it destined to end with another sexual encounter on the banks of the Oldman River? He had been playing the role of the crazy coyote, an animal which saw what it wanted and took it, heedless of the risks and dangers. Yet the spirits seemed to have been offended, for the weather had suddenly turned bad. Had his spirits deserted him, angered in some way by his attack on the Peigan girl?

He soon found that the camp on the slope of Porcupine Hills left him exposed to all the furies of nature's wintery rage. The prayers and holy songs seemingly had no effect as the snow drifted into Charcoal's camp and the biting cold cut through his clothes. It was foolish to stay in the windswept hills when there was protection in the river valleys below. Besides, he had learned that Left Hand and Bear Back Bone had been released from jail; they would give him food and clothing and he would have another chance to kill Red Crow or one of the lesser chiefs.

On the afternoon of 9 November Charcoal left his camp, riding the sorrel racehorse and driving the brown before him. He reasoned that none of his enemies would be searching for him in the bitter cold and heavy snow; they would be warm and comfortable, close to their iron stoves. Striking the headwaters of Beaver Creek, he followed the streambed down toward the river until he found a grove of trees where he could make a fire and shelter for the night.

It was a grave mistake. The Peigans, realizing that Charcoal was still in the area, had not given up their patrols; instead, they discovered the tracks of his two ponies leading from the hills to an isolated part of the reserve. The Indians notified Constable Hatfield at the Peigan Agency who went with the scouts and followed the trail as far as Beaver Creek. As it was dangerous and frustrating to follow a trail at night, the party returned to the agency at sunset, intending to take up the search the following day. At this point in the search, they had no assurance that the tracks even belonged to Charcoal; this might be another of the many false leads they had pursued during the weeks of patrols.

Early next morning, Constable Hatfield set out with an armed detail of determined Peigans. There was Cross Chief, whose wife had been raped; Commodore, who had been shot at by Charcoal; Big Face Chief, whose house the renegade had approached; Many Chiefs, Running Among Buffalo, and Jack Spear, who owned the best racehorse in the party.[1]

Discovering the remains of Charcoal's overnight camp, the men were sure they were on the trail of the outlaw. It led down to the Oldman River, midway between the agency and Legrandeur's ranch, then headed south across the prairies. When it reached the trail to Pincher Creek, it disappeared among the other tracks, throwing the party into confusion. Realizing that their quarry could not be far ahead, Hatfield sent Big Face Chief to Pincher Creek, ten miles away, urging that a patrol be sent to cut him off in case he was heading for the mountains. Later, the keen-eyed scouts picked up the trail again and were off to the south, leaving the constable far behind. Within a few hours the searchers were spread out along the route, with Jack Spear on his powerful gray leading the cavalcade.

When Big Face Chief brought the news to Pincher Creek, Sgt. W. B. Wilde ordered a patrol to mount up. A short time later, the sergeant, riding a large black horse, led his men southeast to cut off the fleeing man. With him were Constable Ambrose, interpreter Charles Holloway, Big Face Chief, New Robe, and a Blood scout, Tail Feathers.

The patrol had traveled for twenty miles through snow six to eight inches deep before it intercepted Charcoal's trail along a tiny creek. The track led to a farmhouse, which had been broken into, and from there to a haystack where horses had recently been fed. As they were now on Dry Fork, only a few miles from the Waterton River, Constable Ambrose was sent to the Kootenai detachment for reinforcements.

Sure that they were close to their quarry, Wilde ordered his men not to take any chances with their lives. If they got within fifty yards of Charcoal they were first to demand that he halt, and if he didn't, they were to shoot him. "If he's going to kill anybody," said the sergeant, "it'll be me."[2]

Charcoal was in the bottom of Dry Fork, cooking some food over a small fire when he saw the patrol at the top of the hill only 400 yards away. Singing his war song, the Indian jumped to the saddle of his sorrel, leaving the other horse and the supplies behind. In a moment his tired animal was up the side of the snow-covered coulee, heading southwest towards the trees that dotted the low hills.

This time he had made his move too late. Some of the search party from the Peigan Reserve had by now caught up with Wilde and the others. The Indians' ponies were worn out after ploughing through snow all morning, but doggedly they pursued the elusive outlaw.

"Come back, my friend," shouted Many Chiefs to Charcoal. "No harm will come to you!"[3]

Momentarily the fugitive stopped, but then he heard the voice of Commodore, the man he had tried to shoot. "Charcoal!" he yelled, "You're now going to find out that it doesn't pay to be crazy!"[4]

Realizing that the Indians, if not the police, were there to kill him, the hunted man urged his sorrel across the prairie. Behind him, Jack Spear, with the finest racer on the Peigan Reserve, rapidly overtook him; soon he was only 150 yards away. At that moment, Charcoal turned in his saddle and stared at the approaching Indian; Spear hurriedly reined back until there was a safe distance between them. Twice the Peigan drew near his quarry, and each time he pulled away after a deadly glance from Charcoal.

As the others caught up, Tail Feathers urged Spear to let him take his horse, but the Peigan refused. All the horses were tiring now, even Charcoal's, so Holloway, Tail Feathers, and Spear dismounted to open fire at the fleeing man. Holloway pulled the trigger of his Lee-Metford carbine, but the extreme cold had congealed the oil on the striker spring, and the gun misfired. A second attempt had the same result. Meanwhile, Spear fired two wild shots with his revolver while Tail Feathers got off a single shot.

"You're not going to get away!" Holloway shouted at the fleeing Indian.

"You're not going to take anything back but my body!" yelled Charcoal.[5] He did not want to die before he had killed a chief, but if they killed him now, it would be a warrior's death, and they would not get his spirit. It would go to the Sand Hills, perhaps not in the way that he had wanted but at least without the humiliation of a white man's rope around his neck.

By this time, Sergeant Wilde had caught up with the Indian pursuers. Their ponies were almost used up, but his big black was strong and fresh. The policeman scooped up the revolver from Tail Feathers and galloped off in pursuit of his prey, who by now had turned due west towards the mountains.

The space between the hunter and the hunted grew smaller and smaller as Wilde's powerful black overtook Charcoal's tired sorrel. Anxiously the Indian looked back as he saw the policeman, revolver in hand and rifle in its scabbard, bearing down upon him. Frightened, he waved the man back but Wilde pressed on, until he was within a few feet of his quarry.

"He's going to kill me," thought Charcoal desperately.[6]

Swinging around in his saddle, the Indian raised his rifle and fired directly at the policeman. Unbelieving, Wilde reeled back, his body hanging briefly on the saddle, then dropped to the ground.

In that instant of flying snow, galloping hooves, waving guns and flying clothes, Charcoal caught sight of a flash of gold. In disbelief he reined up his tired mount and trotted back to the wounded man. Yes. There they were on his sleeve. Three stripes. A chief!

Bursting into a victory song, Charcoal dismounted, gazed calmly down at the sergeant, who was lying on his back, then fired a second shot into his body. The policeman was dead in an instant; at last Charcoal had his spirit messenger. When Sergeant Wilde, resplendent in his scarlet uniform and gold stripes, entered the land of the dead, everyone would be impressed. They would ask how he had died, and he would say that Charcoal had shot him. Now, when Charcoal and his wife took that last long walk, he would be welcomed to the spirit world, where he would remain forever as a great leader and holy man. He had won!

The other pursuers were less than a half mile away, but Charcoal had to finish his mission; now more than ever, he wanted to kill his faithless wife, just as he had vowed. Mounting the policeman's black horse, Charcoal galloped off to the west, over the nearest hill, towards the tree-covered slopes of the mountains.

Perhaps the spirits hadn't deserted him after all. The weather had turned cold and the Indians had found his trail, but the spirits had delivered a chief to him, a white chief. There was no doubt this time; Charcoal knew the man was dead. Not only that, but he had the policeman's horse and rifle, besides his own reliable Winchester.

The news was flashed to Major Steele, then to headquarters in Regina, and on to the prime minister in Ottawa. Sergeant William Brock Wilde, a Mounted Policeman, had been shot and killed.

Exactly one month earlier, the prime minister had been reassured that the police did "not anticipate anything serious" to result from Charcoal's troubles on the Blood Reserve. It was just another case of an Indian breaking the law and running away. Even during the weeks of the manhunt, there was considerable sympathy expressed for the outlaw and admiration for the way he had eluded the police.

But now that all changed.

Sergeant Wilde, a gruff, mustached giant of a man, was dead. A popular soldier, he had been in the Royal Irish Dragoon Guards for seven years before emigrating to Canada and joining the Mounted Police in 1882. Like Major Steele, he was "a typical British soldier,"[7] a fearless authoritarian who had been at home among the English ranchers at Pincher Creek. He had been a familiar and impressive sight as he rode scarlet-clad down the main street with his two hounds at his heels.

Perhaps he drank too much at times, getting demoted from staff sergeant to sergeant in 1892 and to corporal a year later, but he had been working his way up through the ranks again at the time of his death. His promotion back to sergeant had taken place two years earlier, in 1894. Otherwise, his record in the force had generally been good. In 1883, he had demonstrated his bravery when he had ordered Chief Piapot to move his tepee from the railway right-of-way near Maple Creek. When the Cree chief had refused, the policeman calmly began to pull the lodge down, in spite of rifles being fired over his head and knives waved about him.

"Piapot had either to kill the corporal," said an observer at the time, "stick his knife into the heart of the whole British nation by the murder of this unruffled soldier, or give in and move away."[8] He chose the latter, and British justice triumphed.

When Wilde died in his brave but futile attempt to capture Charcoal, it was as though he had acted on behalf of the whole British Empire. He was upholding a trust, serving justice, and bringing civilization to the wilderness. "The British empire," said an admirer of the dead sergeant, "is held together by the existence of such heroes, and by the brave deeds which characterize such lives. It would be as impossible for such a man, no matter what the danger that menaced, to act the coward and shirk his duty, as it would be for the coward to perform it."[9]

Yet even Major Steele wondered why Wilde had tried to capture the armed desperado, especially after he had cautioned his men to take no chances and to shoot if he did not surrender after a warning. And if Wilde had been intent on capturing the man, why had he ridden straight for the barrel of Charcoal's gun? If he had approached from the other side, Charcoal would have found it necessary to raise the rifle and turn it around or else wheel his horse to face his pursuer. Either way, the sergeant, with revolver in hand, would have had time to shoot first. As it was, he had ridden directly toward his death.

Sergeant Wilde's bravery could not be questioned. His strategy and judgment may have been weak but they had apparently been based on the decision to take the man alive. It was a commendable, but fatal, choice. Instead of repeating the heroic act of 1883, bluffing an Indian into submission, he had ended his life crumpled on the snow-covered prairies.

As soon as the others reached Wilde's body, Holloway got his rifle in working order and fired two quick shots at the fleeing killer. Meanwhile, Tail Feathers grabbed the sorrel which Charcoal had abandoned, took the Lee-Metford rifle, and rode off alone in pursuit of his fellow tribesman.

Tail Feathers and Charcoal were about the same age, belonged to the same age-grade society, and had been friends all their lives. But Tail Feathers was a regular Mounted Police scout, not just an Indian who had been pressed into service for fifty cents a day. In his years at the Standoff and Pincher Creek detachments he had gone on patrols with the red coats, eaten with them, slept in their camps. The dead sergeant was not simply a white man; he was a fellow member of the force.

As he topped the rise on the nearby hill, Tail Feathers could see the fugitive about a mile ahead. He pressed the sorrel down into the valley and across the plain, but the animal was worn out. Staggering slightly, it finally came to a dead stop.

Looking around, Tail Feathers saw a number of cowboys from the Geddes ranch and begged them to give him a fresh horse. They all refused, saying their animals were too wild to ride, but the foreman gave the Indian a note to take to the ranch headquarters. Disappointed, for his quarry was only a short distance ahead, Tail Feathers walked to the ranch, arriving too late in the day to resume the pursuit.

Meanwhile, Wilde's body was loaded onto Holloway's horse and carried six miles to the Thibaudeau ranch on the North Fork; from there it was taken by wagon to Pincher Creek and later received a Masonic, military, hero's funeral in Macleod.

Upon receipt of the news about the killing, Major Steele sent Inspector Sanders and all available men to join the manhunt. In spite of the intense, thirty-below cold, the police made a rapid march to Kootenai detachment, arriving the following afternoon. There they were split into three parties. One was sent up Dry Fork with Sergeant Watson, another up North Fork with Sanders, and a third to Big Bend under Sergeant Bertles.

On the Blood Reserve, the message from Major Steele arrived the next morning, 11 November. The news quickly spread throughout the camps, and within two hours, more than fifty armed Bloods were gathered, ready for action. Without the help of police, they searched the river bottom for fresh trails, following two false tracks, even rushing down upon a startled constable who

144

was carrying news of the killing to the Big Bend detachment. At nightfall, scouts were placed all along the river near the camps of Red Crow and Left Hand.

At Pincher Creek, ex-policeman John Herron heard about the killing at one o'clock on the morning of 11 November. He immediately called a meeting of local ranchers, at which James Foote, T. Craig, and John Thibaudeau agreed on forming a posse to help in the hunt. They were on the road before dawn, joined en route by another rancher named Hugh Leaper, and reached the Geddes ranch at daybreak. There they found Tail Feathers, who told them what had happened and led them up the trail towards the mountains. They were well along the route, near the North Fork, by the time Sanders reached the mouth of that stream and began searching in the same direction as the posse, but behind them, from the east.

With Tail Feathers in the lead, the ranchers rapidly followed the clear trail until they reached heavy timber. There the tracks disappeared, so the party split, the Indian, Thibaudeau, and Herron following the ridge and the others staying in the valley. Farther along, those on the ridge moved over to the south branch of the stream and down through its gully. They were just beginning to mount the hill on the opposite side when Tail Feathers noticed a movement in the trees above them.

The searchers had been on the fugitive's trail all day, and already the long shadows of evening were making the hunt difficult. Riding back to a small rise, Tail Feathers found a clear view across the valley. There, standing in front of Wilde's black horse was Charcoal, his gun leveled in their direction.

Quickly the three pursuers dismounted and crouched behind the trees. Tail Feathers crawled over to a tree stump, took aim, and pressed the trigger. The damned Lee-Metford jammed again, just as it had for Charles Holloway. He tried a second time with the same luck. Then, while Tail Feathers called out to Charcoal to surrender, Herron worked himself into a good position and fired ten or twelve rounds with his revolver. But the outlaw was at least 300 yards away, and none of the bullets found its mark. By this time, Tail Feathers had finally dislodged the frozen spring in his carbine and fired two shots across the valley, but by then the Indian had disappeared back into the trees.

The shooting brought the rest of the party to the scene, and while the others searched the valley, Tail Feathers and Hugh Leaper crossed the creek bed and went up the slope, hoping to catch Charcoal in an open meadow on the ridge. They were too slow, however, for the fugitive had disappeared. It was dark now, the temperature hovering around thirty-five below, so the posse decided to split into two groups for the night, one making the

145

fifteen-mile ride to the Geddes ranch and the other heading for the Glasgow ranch. The next day they would meet the Mounted Police patrols and continue the search.

Charcoal had not fired a shot during the whole encounter on the south branch.

Chapter seventeen

A chilling frost hung in the air. The trees were weighed down by new snow, and the rocks sat frigidly, under little caps of white. There was a stark stillness to the world as Charcoal rode down from the hills. The animals were all secure in their hiding places, except for a few range cattle huddled in the coulees. Not even the snowy owl uttered its nightly whoo as it prowled in search of food.

The spirit voices were muted, too, as though driven into their ghostly places by the onslaught of winter. The only moving figure that night was a crazy coyote, hungry, hunted, alone. His food was gone; his extra horse with his blankets was lost. All he had were his two rifles, a butcher knife, and field glasses. For clothes he had a shirt, trousers, moccasins, a fur cap with coyote-skin earflaps, and a red Hudson's Bay blanket coat held in place with a cartridge belt. He had nineteen bullets, five taken from the policeman's Lee-Metford, the rest for the Winchester.

That was enough.

After weeks of traveling, hiding, taunting his enemy, he had at last accomplished his mission: he had killed a chief. Now all he needed to do was to find his faithless wife so they could travel together to the Sand Hills.

The days had taken their toll on Charcoal. Thin and emaciated, he was more and more like his gaunt, four-footed namesake. This is what happened when a coyote went crazy. It was so busy biting its own tail or attacking its enemies that it didn't take time to eat. Its fur became matted, its body thin, its mouth full of cuts and sores from trying to eat foolish food. Sometimes its moccasins wore out, or it became insensitive to the cold as it barked at the moon or prayed to its unseen spirits. It traveled silently at night, loping across the plains, leading its horse into enemy camps, driving the Indian dogs away in fear. It laughed at danger, howled from the hills, doubled back on its trails, and when it was ready, it struck to kill.

Oh, coyotes are crazy,
They catch what they want.
Hai ya, hai ya, ho!

His pursuers were still back in the hills when Charcoal crossed the ice of the Waterton River and rode toward the Blood Reserve. With the help of his brothers, he would find Pretty Wolverine Woman before dawn and kill her. The moon was overhead, and the stars covered Charcoal's world like a huge glimmering bowl as he crossed the Cochrane lease. By now Wilde's black horse was tired and stumbling after a day and a half of steady riding. This time, Charcoal didn't wait to find a good racehorse. Stopping near Big Road's cabin, he took a pinto cayuse from the shed, changed saddles, and was on his way downstream towards his brothers' camp.

Each night after they had been released from jail, Left Hand and Bear Back Bone had obediently uncovered their windows and lit their lamps to let Charcoal know they were at home. Not far away, in the trees, scouts stood ready and waiting for their call. During the day, Left Hand had gone to the buttes to search the valley with his field glasses or to signal with his mirror, just in case Charcoal was near.

As each day passed, Bear Back Bone had become more and more concerned; if his brother weren't captured before 12 November, Crane Chief would go on trial as scheduled. That was the agreement. Now only one night remained, and already Judge Rouleau was in Macleod for the fall sittings of the supreme court. There were four cases on the docket: Sam Sansavore charging Joe Gregoire with stealing his horse; the Queen versus Dowson, who was charged with wounding; a civil case against the Town of Macleod; and the Queen versus Crane Chief and his friends. The lawyer had advised the Indians to plead guilty and to throw themselves upon the mercy of the court. The testimony of the disaffected member of their gang provided an iron-clad case against them. Only one hope remained.

Cautiously Charcoal approached the Choking camp. He had traveled more than seventy miles, circling, doubling back, hiding his trail. Now, with sunrise only an hour or two away, he needed food and rest.

It was good to have brothers. Left Hand had been his leader since they were children. Tough, aggressive, and a real warrior, he had gone into battle fearlessly to attack the Crees. He had defied the elders in making war against their enemies. He had been in the Horn Society with Charcoal and Bear Back Bone. Together they had participated in the holy rites as they had smoked the pipe, burned the incense, chanted the songs.

Even now Charcoal knew his brothers would be there to guide and help him. He was almost at the end of his journey; all he asked were food, rest, and information about his wife. In an hour, perhaps two, it would all be over; his physical body could be thrown away while his warrior spirit would go to the land of the dead. As the days passed, he had given himself over more and more to the spirit world, his only links with reality being his rifle and his brothers. If everything and everyone else deserted him, these would remain his friends until his work was done.

There was silence in the camp and, curiously, a pale light in Left Hand's cabin. Like his coyote brother, Charcoal was suspicious of anything out of the ordinary; to keep a lamp lit at four o'clock in the morning was not normal. The Indian circled the cabin, watching for signs of movement, looking for a trap. Perhaps the cabin was filled with policemen, not his brothers. Yet the snow revealed only a few scattered tracks of moccasined feet, no heavy bootprints nor the marks of many scouts.

Tying his pinto to a tree about fifty yards away, Charcoal walked silently to the cabin and knocked. No answer. He knocked again. As the door slowly swung open, the fugitive relaxed for a moment when he saw the familiar face of his brother, Left Hand. Then the muscles of his face tightened, his eyes narrowed, and his voice was flat and hard.

"You have betrayed me!"[1]

Left Hand, his own brother, was standing before him fully clothed in the middle of the night. He was waiting to trap him!

Quickly Charcoal turned and dashed to his horse, his brother following at his heels.

"There's no use," Left Hand called. "Mr. Steele and Mr. Wilson told me you'd better give yourself up. It'll be better for you!"

"No, I won't. I'm going on."[2]

Left Hand wrapped his arms around his brother, pulling him away from the horse. At this first act of violence, Charcoal tried to raise his rifle but the brother called for help; moments later Left Hand's wife and Bear Back Bone were upon the desperate man, tearing away his rifle, grabbing his butcher knife, and wrestling him to the ground.

In dismay Charcoal struggled with his brothers. He had beaten the police, the scouts, the ranchers, everyone. Of all people, his brothers understood his mission, his need to kill a chief and his faithless wife. They knew about his wish to go to the Sand Hills as a leader, and they realized what would happen to his spirit if the police captured and hanged him.

This thing couldn't be happening! He felt his body being pushed and dragged through the snow toward the cabin; his arms pinioned at his sides; his sister-in-law, his fat sister-in-law, sitting squarely on his shoulders. It was no dream; it was real.

At that moment, his rifle gone, betrayed by his brothers, Charcoal surrendered to the real world. "I give up," he said to Left Hand. "Now you can be a chief for catching me."[3]

All fight left him as he lay on the earthen floor, a tired and beaten man. He heard his brother shout for White Buffalo Chief, Big Plume, and Willie Red Crow to help him, that he had captured Charoal. A little later, White Man Left, Calf Chief, and Chief Moon arrived, curiously watching their onetime friend who now lay before them like a gaunt, trapped animal.

Charcoal was allowed to sit in a chair, and there, huddled down with his hood pulled over his head, the exhausted man appeared to sleep while waiting for the police to come from Standoff. There was no hope now of killing Pretty Wolverine Woman; in fact, Left Hand had told him the police had locked her up in Macleod. Cautiously, with a movement so slight that it scarcely disturbed his winter coat, Charcoal grasped an awl which was hidden in his clothes. He didn't want this body any longer; his brothers could have it. The sharp point of the awl pierced through the skin of his arm and into a vein. And again.

Chief Moon, sitting on a woodpile near the door, saw something moving on the floor. It looked like a dark, dirt-covered worm.

"What's that?" he asked.

"Where?"[4]

When they raised Charcoal's coat to discover what was causing the shifting soil, they saw a sprawling pool of blood under his chair. When his coat was pulled back, the blood came spurting from his arm. Charcoal weakly tried to push them away, but they covered his wounds with flour and bound them with strips of cotton.

Why didn't they let him die?

Even the coyote, after it had taunted its last dog, stolen its last food, killed its last enemy was allowed to die as it wished. It might crawl into a cave, be torn apart by a savage pack of dogs, or even be destroyed by its own kind. Charcoal's adventure was over and he wanted to die; he was ready to abandon this world in which no one wanted him to stay.

Why didn't they let him die?

Chapter eighteen

Charcoal was weak from the loss of blood but still alive when Sgt. W. B. Macleod arrived at Left Hand's house. The policeman's first action was to take possession of the prisoner's meager possessions: one regulation police saddle and bridle, a Lee-Metford carbine number 39, a pair of field glasses, butcher knife and sheath, cartridge belt and ammunition. And one awl.

Left Hand obligingly hitched a team of horses to his wagon and helped transport his brother down to the detachment. It was bitterly cold, so they stopped to warm themselves at the Catholic mission, where a priest with medical training examined the prisoner. He declared that Charcoal was fit to travel, that his wounds were not mortal ones. By dawn, 11 November, the Indian was behind bars in the police outpost.

Now Charcoal withdrew almost completely from the real world. Although weak and emaciated, he would not eat and had to be force fed. He answered no one but lay as though in a trance. On the following day, when he was being taken to Macleod, Charcoal was met and examined by the police surgeon. "He is apparently in a very unstrung nervous condition," reported the doctor, "but his pulse which is fairly quiet and regular would indicate that this is either 'put on' or will shortly pass off. It is not improbable that he is purposely trying to act in a 'crazy' manner."[1]

They still didn't understand. Had they never seen a wild coyote, worn out, trapped, thrown into a cage? It lay there, its eyes glazed, its mind numbed, only its body refusing to die. If they left it long enough without forcing it to eat, the captured animal would perish.

Charcoal now belonged to the spirit world, but his body would not let him go. His mind was walking along that shadowy path to the Sand Hills, the path that the policeman had taken two days before. Already they must know about Charcoal, be expecting him.

When the police wagon arrived in Macleod, Major Steele met Charcoal for the first time. This exhausted, sickly, unimpressive little man had eluded, outsmarted, and beaten his men at every turn. The strategies and maneuvers of the military-minded officer had come to naught; only trickery and duplicity had finally resulted in bringing him to bay.

Charcoal's skill and his endurance had been remarkable, mused Steele. Many people had admired him, right up to the time he had killed Sergeant Wilde. After that, he had been hunted by everyone, the police, ranchers, Indians, yet it had still taken his own brothers to bring him in.

At the barracks, Charcoal was not put in the cells but was placed in the main guardroom, his shackles chained firmly to the floor. His bed was a low platform. As he lay there all but motionless, three police guards kept a day-and-night watch. Even when he was half-carried to the toilet, the men stayed at his side, giving him opportunity neither to escape nor commit suicide.

The only times that life came back into Charcoal's eyes were on the few occasions when Indians came to see him. They weren't really visitors but prisoners whom he had known in happier times. One was his old friend Little Leaf, to whom he told his adventures of the previous weeks.

"Don't complain about being in jail," Charcoal told him. "You will only be here for a little while, but the police are going to kill me."[2]

He brightened up too, but in a different way, when the Indian agent came to discuss his will. Instantly, Charcoal insisted that the medicine bundle from the Holy Women's Society was his; he had paid ten horses for it. He wanted Agent Wilson to send it to some museum in the East so that his wife could never again perform its sacred rituals. Obligingly, a clause to this effect was placed in the prisoner's will.

But these flashes of life were rare. The real world was not his anymore. He had given it up, thrown it away. Only his brothers and the police were preventing him from leaving it.

A reporter who was permitted to visit Charcoal described the scene. When the journalist entered, "the prisoner was being held in a sitting posture on a platform on which he sleeps. He appears to be in the last stages of consumption, to which disease all his family are victims. His sickness however is more apparent than real. Ever since his capture he has seemed to be in a state of utter collapse, but the police are convinced that it is mostly sham. He pretends to be unable to walk or even to sit upright. He keeps his eyes closed and is seemingly quite helpless and in a semi-unconscious state."[3]

The periodic reports of the surgeon confirmed his condition, but the Mounted Police obviously preferred to believe he was faking.

"When being spoken to or roused to take food," said the doctor, "he acts in the same nervous manner as before, but I am still of the opinion that this is put on."[4] A few days later the surgeon added that Charcoal "can understand what is said to him by the Interpreter and that he is fit to undergo the preliminary examination."[5] Proceedings began on 1 December. The next day, "He was taken across to the Courtroom . . . [in the] morning and again . . . [in the] afternoon and for the most part acted in the same manner as before. When, however, the last witness was called, viz, Charcoal's wife, he showed that he was able to understand."[6]

A few weeks later at his trial, Charcoal admitted killing the boy and the sergeant, but denied everything else. He said he had not shot at McNeil, but others had heard him confess. He claimed his family had gone willingly with him, but Young Pine refuted him. He said he had not been to Legrandeur's, but the woman could identify him. He argued that Wilde had shot at him first, but the policeman's gun was unfired.

For most of the trial, Charcoal sat watching the proceedings in a trance-like state as though he were a disinterested onlooker, unchanging in his expression, unable to stand or move about without help.

When the testimony had been completed, the jury took only eight minutes to render a verdict.

"You have been found guilty of the charges of killing Medicine Pipe Stem and Sgt. Wilde," Judge Scott informed the prisoner. "You have received a fair trial on both charges. Having been found guilty, it is my duty to pass sentence upon you. There is only one sentence that the law allows me and that sentence is death. I cannot hold out any hope of clemency on the part of the Crown. You must, therefore, prepare to meet your Maker.

"The sentence of the Court is that you be taken from here to the guard room of the barracks at Macleod, and kept there until the 16th day of March next, and that, on that day, you be taken from there to the place of execution and be hanged by the neck until you are dead, and may the Lord have mercy on your soul."[7]

In the two months between the trial and the execution, Charcoal remained helpless, lethargic, and aloof from the guardroom, the barracks, the town around him. The curious came, some to stare, some to photograph, some to talk about the white man's way of life. They didn't understand that he had rejected their ways, their codes, and their laws when he had decided to become an Indian again, like his forefathers. A Protestant missionary asked him if he knew about the Bible and salvation.

153

Charcoal admitted that the Anglican teacher, Mr. Mills, had at times visited his cabin to speak of such things to him. Later, a black-robed priest, Emile Legal, also came to inquire about Charcoal's soul.

The Oblate father had been laboring among the Bloods for ten years with little success. "The middle-aged Indians still cling to their old religious belief," said Agent Wilson, "and the younger ones do not manifest much interest in religion of any kind."[8] Under normal circumstances, a holy man like Charcoal, the owner of medicine bundles and religious objects, would have been the last person the priest would have approached. But the situation had changed; soon he would need the everlasting succor of Jesus Christ.

Day after day, Father Legal visited the prisoner, counseling, talking, and praying. Charcoal heard his voice, accepted his friendship, and obligingly learned to follow some of the simple hymns. Later, Legal claimed that Charcoal had been converted, that he had accepted Christianity. Although the good people of Macleod were pleased to hear of the eleventh-hour conversion, the likelihood of Charcoal casting aside his native beliefs was the same as for a coyote turning into a lamb. Charcoal had accepted the priest's friendly visits, but his whole life and his impending death were so closely intertwined with his own beliefs that they could never have been discarded. Rather, the prisoner had simply nodded his head in agreement to please the black robe.

Charcoal knew what his fate would be if he accepted the white man's religion and rejected his own. Such a thing had happened several times before. On one occasion a man had accepted Christianity and had discarded his medicine bundles. When he died, he went to the white man's heaven but was told no Indians were there. Next, he went to the Sand Hills but was not allowed to enter, for he had turned his back on the Indian way. Despairing, the man had no choice but to return to life; there he renounced his Christian teachings and went back to his former religion.

In Charcoal's mind, his eternal life was assured only if his spirit could avoid being trapped by the white man. If his body was hanged, his spirit might go to the Sand Hills in shame, but his ghostly messenger would already have reported his deeds. That would count for something.

On the other hand, if he let the white man take his body and bury it in the ground, his spirit would be trapped with the underground people and lost forever.

He had come so far! When he shot the boy, he had decided to throw his life away; if he had killed Farmer McNeil instead of wounding him, the ordeal would have been over weeks earlier. But luck had been against him: a flower had deflected his first bullet; a badly held lantern had caused him to miss the policeman at Cardston. Then his wife had escaped. But just when he had thought the spirits might have deserted him, he had triumphed. He should have stayed and died fighting after the killing of Wilde but he had desperately wanted to take his wife on the long last journey. That, too, had been a mistake.

In the end, however, he seemed to have gained more than he had lost. Even with a rope around his neck, he could go to the Sand Hills with the knowledge that the policeman had already been there, telling the ghostly ones the name of the man who had killed him. Perhaps Wilde had continued on to the spirit world of the white man, but at least he would have carried the message on his way.

Now only one step remained: to be placed on some lonely hill near the Belly Buttes where his spirit could wander for a few days among the camps, trees, and coulees. Then it would go east, how far he did not know, until it met the others from the spirit world; they would ask his name, invite him to their camps, listen to his adventures and take him to hunt the spirit buffalo.

To be assured of his future existence, Charcoal asked the police if his body could be turned over to his relatives after the execution. Goose Chief, who had been arrested for supplying the gun which killed Sergeant Wilde, had played no part in the betrayal. He would know what to do.

Inquiries were made, and Major Steele was able to inform the prisoner that an order had been received from the Lieutenant-Governor of the North West Territories decreeing that after it was all over, his body would be "handed over to the relatives of the deceased for burial."[9]

In the days before the hanging, a scaffold was built in the horse corral near the barracks. Crow Eagle, the Peigan head chief, and Heard Before, a Blood Indian, were included in the group of newspapermen, officials, and others on hand for the event. Police ringed the entire area in case some last-minute attempt were made to free the prisoner or, with coyote-like cunning, Charcoal tried to escape.

But the prisoner's body was the only part of him still in the real world; the rest had retreated into its own secret place, waiting for the spirit to be set free. As they left the guardroom on the fateful day, Charcoal began to sing the high, piercing strains of his holy song, but Father Legal, who was at his side, stopped him. Unable to walk, the Indian was loaded onto a wagon, driven to the scaffold, and carried up the last few steps toward eternity. His body, having no will of its own, was not even capable of standing, so a chair was placed over the trapdoor, a white cloth draped over his head, and the noose placed round his neck.

He had known. He had known when he killed the boy in the cowshed that if the police caught him, they would put a rope around his neck. He had been right; it was happening.

At eight minutes past eight, on the morning of 16 March 1897, John Smith pulled the lever which took the life of the murderer Charcoal, alias Lazy Young Man, alias The Palate.

After he was declared officially dead, Charcoal's body was given to Father Legal to take to the Blood Reserve. When the priest's wagon stopped in front of the mission house late in the afternoon, about twenty Indians, including the brothers, were waiting. At the insistence of one of the chiefs, the lid of the coffin was pried off so they could be sure that Charcoal's body was really inside. Already a rumor had spread that he had been brought back to life in the form of a grizzly bear which would wreak vengeance upon the whole camp. Yet all the Indians saw was the gaunt body of a man who had once been their friend.

According to the orders of the Lieutenant-Governor, the body was to be turned over to the family for their native burial. But Father Legal made it clear that he had no intentions of giving up the remains of Charcoal. He claimed that the Indian had become a convert to Christianity while in jail and that he must be buried in consecrated ground. Then, contrary of everyone's wishes, a grave was dug in the little Catholic cemetery and the coffin lowered into the dark, frozen ground.

The ultimate, awful fate that Charcoal had feared in life had become a reality in death. After weeks of running, fighting, and hiding, he had finally found a worthy courier to send to the land of the dead. When the red-coated messenger had arrived there, it had proclaimed: "Charcoal has killed me; he will be following behind." The spirits in the Sand Hills had nodded their ghostly heads and murmured to themselves that the messenger, a white man with three stripes on his coat, was indeed an important leader. Therefore the name he uttered must be that of a man even greater than he. Thus the way had been prepared for the great warrior. But his spirit would never come. It was trapped beneath the earth in a white man's coffin, trapped forever with underground spirits.

The white man never understood.

Epilogue

After the great manhunt each person involved went on to pick up the threads of his life. Even while Charcoal still languished in jail, Major Steele weathered a crisis of his own. While being publicly acclaimed for the capture of Charcoal, Steele was in deep trouble over his silver mines. When the commissioner learned about the major's involvement in the private speculation, the matter went all the way to the prime minister's desk. Disturbed by the possible implications of policemen investing in their commanding officer's mine, the commissioner directed Steele to explain his actions.

"I have never asked any N.C.O. or Constable in the Force to join me in any speculation whatever," Steele said defensively. "I had pointed out to one or two officers in the Force that the group of claims were for sale but only on account of their having previously asked me to let them know if any good opportunities offered themselves."[1]

He admitted that a number of policemen had bought shares but emphatically denied that he had solicited their support. "Staff Sgt. Hilliard paid for an interest in the group, the money being transmitted through me, and I understand that a few of the men purchased a small interest through him."[2]

The prime minister was not impressed. Word came down from his office that "whilst he has no wish to interfere in any way with private investments, he deems it undesirable that members of the Force should engage in the active management of mining ventures, and he hopes that Supt. Steele and Insp. Jarvis will retire from the board of the Ibex Mining Company as soon as they can."[3]

Steele ignored the directive, but a few months later the whole matter was resolved when a world collapse of silver prices left most of the investors with little more than a bitter memory. The money they had put into Ibex, Supt. R. B. Deane observed, "we had far better have kept in our pockets."[4]

157

But before the bubble had burst, Major Steele was off to uphold the Queen's law in the far north. The Klondike gold rush had electrified the world in 1897, sending thousands of gold seekers crowding the boats and trails to the Yukon. Fears were expressed that the lawlessness of the nearby American camps would spill over into Canadian territory, so extra police were dispatched to the north. Steele was placed in charge of the mountain passes, with headquarters at Lake Bennett. His task was to supervise the thousands of prospectors trying to cross the White and Chilkoot passes in the winter of 1897-98.

With the British flag flying overhead, Steele worked from morning to night, settling disputes, collecting customs duties, interviewing miners, and maintaining law and order. So successful was his work that no major crimes were committed and a peaceful flotilla set sail for the gold fields in the spring. In recognition of his work, Steele was placed in command of the Mounted Police in the entire gold-rush area and appointed a member of the Yukon Territorial Council. Joining him in his work were Inspectors Primrose and Jarvis, partners in the search for Charcoal.

In 1899, when Britain went to war against the Boers in South Africa, Steele volunteered to raise a mounted corps from the prairies. When his offer was accepted, he resigned from the Mounted Police to become a colonel in the Canadian army. In the next few weeks, he raised three squadrons of mounted riflemen from western Canada to form a corps which was christened Lord Strathcona's Horse. Overseas, they proved to be excellent horsemen and even better fighters. Colonel Steele, the patriotic warhorse, was in his glory. His corps won the respect of British regulars as time after time their knowledge of prairie life proved invaluable on the veld.

"We entered Standerton unopposed," said Steele as he recalled one incident, "welcomed by large numbers of British people, who waved handkerchiefs and hats, calling out, 'Welcome, Canadians!' "[5]

When the war was over, the colonel could say proudly, "We saw much fighting, and I think proved that from the Dominion came as good fighting men as ever played at the great game of war."[6] As in the pursuit of Charcoal, the strategy and maneuvers of combat were, for Steele, a giant chess game, with its human kings, knights, and pawns.

In London after the war, Colonel Steele was presented to King George V at Buckingham Palace, where he was given the Victorian Order, his men receiving South African War medals. When offering the monarch's colors to the regiment, the King said, "I feel sure in confiding this colour to you, Colonel Steele, and to those under you, that you will always defend it and will do your

158

duty.''[7] Like so many who had carried the flag to British possessions throughout the Empire, "duty" was the word which Steele understood. To him, it was a solemn bond of faith which held the Empire together.

Rather than returning to the North West Mounted Police, Steele accepted the appointment as colonel in the South African Constabulary, a semimilitary corps not unlike the Canadian police. In the mopping up operations after the war, he helped disarm the blacks who were ready to carry on their own fight against the Dutch and established a series of patrols, similar to those which had worked so well in the Canadian West.

Colonel Steele was not impressed with the African blacks. "The Kaffir is not like the Red Indian or Maori," he said, "who in their primitive state are dignified and courteous and will take no liberties."[8]

"The Kaffir as a labourer, in any capacity, is trying," he went on. "Under the influence of fear they will work fairly well, but in gangs it would be an unusual thing to see more than five to ten per cent busy at the same time. As domestics in towns, both men and women are poor servants. . . . Both sexes are by nature untruthful, and few are capable of gratitude for any kind of act. Admonition by the cat-o'-nine-tails is the only thing understood."[9]

In the ensuing months, Steele personally toured the area time and again, meeting Boer farmers, enforcing regulations, and helping the colony to rebuild after the bitter fighting. In 1906, with his wife seriously ill, Steele finally left South Africa to return to western Canada; there he was appointed commanding officer of military district number thirteen, in Calgary. Later he moved to Winnipeg.

In 1914, at the outbreak of World War One, the old Imperial warrior was back in harness with the rank of major-general. Turning to his comrades from the Mounted Police and Boer War, he raised and trained the Second Canadian Division which he took to England in 1915. Although not permitted to go to France because of his age, he assumed command of British and Canadian units in the Shorncliffe area, and in 1918, at the end of the war, he was given a knighthood. Sir Sam Steele, lifelong soldier of the Empire, died in England in the following year.

Considered one of the great Canadians of his time, Steele had maintained a consistent course throughout his life. His duty was towards the Empire; the might and right of British justice was the key to its success. If a man obeyed the law and accepted the principles of British life, well and good. But if he turned his back on the law or if he rejected the principles of the British system, he was a threat to the Empire. This rule applied to a miner in the

Klondike, a black in Africa, or an Indian who tried to follow tribal ways.

Charcoal's world had been entirely foreign to Steele. His was a military life, dominated by regulations, patriotism, and dedication to service. Steele's way was not wrong; he had simply come from a different world.

And what of the others who had taken part in Charcoal's great adventure? Left Hand was given a reward of seventy-five dollars for helping to capture his brother; in 1905 he was appointed a minor chief of the tribe, replacing Moon, from the Many Brown Weasels band. He tried to unite his own band with Moon's clan, but most of the followers rejected him, preferring to join the Fish Eaters.

"The Indians themselves never recognized his authority," recalled a member of the tribe. "In fact, they all adopted a particularly belligerent attitude toward him, believing his act to be unbrotherly in the extreme.... Gambler, a childhood friend of ... [Charcoal], once approached Left Hand, and after hurling at him all the vile epithets he could think of, proceeded to thrash him thoroughly with his whip. Others were about to repeat the punishment but were stopped by timely intervention."[10]

Known to the Indian Department as a hard-working farmer, Left Hand favored a move to surrender part of the reserve and generally supported the programs of the government, rather than those of his tribe. His actions were understandable, for the Bloods never forgave him for his betrayal.

Bear Back Bone, already sick when he helped to capture Charcoal, barely lived long enough to spend his seventy-five dollar prize. In an advanced stage of tuberculosis, he died less than a year later. The Bloods didn't blame him as much as they did Left Hand. They knew he was sick and realized that his son's life was at stake.

True to his word, Major Steele did get Crane Chief off the hook. There wasn't time to delay the court proceedings the morning after the capture, so Crane Chief and the others pleaded guilty. Advised that a deal was being made, Judge Rouleau obligingly withheld sentence until the following day. That evening, Indian Agent Wilson explained to the judge what had happened.

"Under these circumstances," said Wilson, "it was necessary to allow Crane Chief to go free, but as he had been the leader of the party and on more than one occasion previously brought up on this charge, I felt it would not be fair to punish the others, and let Crane Chief go. I therefore ... proposed that he should discharge all the prisoners on suspended sentence, not on account of anything in their own case deserving such favour, but out of a compliment to the Head Chiefs and to show these Indians that the Department, Police and white people in the district appreciated the work they had done in searching for and arresting Charcoal."[11]

Compliment to the head chiefs! It was an outright deal and the judge knew it. He refused to take the responsibility for turning the confessed criminals loose and would do so only if Agent Wilson made a public statement in open court. The report duly appeared in the press.

"Before passing sentence, Mr. James Wilson, Indian agent, addressed His Lordship on behalf of the prisoners, asking that they be allowed to go on suspended sentence. His reason for this was that the father of one of the prisoners had been instrumental in securing Charcoal, and that all the friends of the prisoners had rendered every material assistance to the police in connection with the same matter. He thought this would produce a far better effect than to sentence them to imprisonment.

"His Lordship then addressed the Indians, saying that he had decided to act upon Mr. Wilson's suggestion, and let them go for the present, but that whether they were called up again for sentence would depend altogether upon their future good behaviour."[12]

Crane Chief had learned a bitter lesson. Like his father, he had found that the way of the white man was hard and that there was no place for wild young Indians. Abandoning his nocturnal forays, Crane Chief turned to farming as his way of life.

Tail Feathers, the scout who was still searching the mountains when Charcoal was captured by his family, later suffered a fate similar to that of the hunted man. In the autumn of 1907, Tail Feathers learned that his Sarcee wife was having an affair and decided to kill her. Like Charcoal, he chose to play the role of the crazy coyote, planning to kill the head chief of the Lower Agency, Thunder Chief, before shooting his wife and himself. When he arrived at the village, he discovered that his intended victim was away but was expected back soon. Something about the way he acted caused the chief's wives to become suspicious, so when their husband returned they told him their fears.

Not completely convinced, yet cautious enough to load his revolver, Thunder Chief met Tail Feathers as he rode up to the door. Without saying a word, the scout raised his rifle and shot the chief in the chest. Dropping to a crouch, Thunder Chief returned the fire, killing Tail Feathers instantly. The chief, although mortally wounded, was carried into the house where he lived for several more days.

In the end, the Indians believed, Thunder Chief outwitted his killer. When the spirit of Tail Feathers realized that the chief had

161

not gone ahead to the land of the dead, it was unwilling to make the journey. It stayed around the Blood Reserve for a while, then drifted to its former home on the Blackfoot Reserve. For the next thirty years it wandered restlessly back and forth, perhaps never knowing that Thunder Chief had died.

There were also the six unwilling people who had accompanied Charcoal when he set out from his cabin on 13 October. The oldest stepson died in school two years later, while the daughter, Owl Woman, died in 1906. None of the others lived much longer, none except Pretty Wolverine Woman. She, the cause of the whole tragic saga, outlived them all. Marrying a successful rancher named Black Plume at the turn of the century, she spent the rest of her life as an enigmatic holy woman who would never discuss those few tragic weeks. She died in Cardston at the age of eighty-one, exactly fifty years from the day on which Charcoal was captured. She had been given an extra half century because her husband had failed in his mission.

Notes

CHAPTER ONE

1. Hugh A. Dempsey, *A Blackfoot Winter Count,* p.12.
2. Interviews with Suzette Eagle Ribs, 21 April 1974 and John Yellowhorn, 14 August 1974.
3. Letter, S. B. Steele to R. L. Galbraith, 19 October 1896, Steele Papers, Glenbow-Alberta Institute.

CHAPTER TWO

1. *The Macleod Gazette,* 14 July 1883.
2. Interview with Jim White Bull, 22 July 1954.

CHAPTER THREE

1. Paraphrased from Mike Mountain Horse, "Charcoal and How He Grew Blacker," p. 66. Also see court testimony of Yellow Creek, "Queen vs. Charcoal," Section I, p.5.
2. Testimony of Yellow Creek, "Queen vs. Charcoal," Section I, p.6.
3. Ibid.
4. Testimony of Pretty Wolverine Woman, "Queen vs. Charcoal," Section I, p.13, and testimony of Owl Woman, "Queen vs. Charcoal," Section III, pp.8-9.
5. Ibid.
6. Testimony of Owl Woman, "Queen vs. Charcoal," Section III, p.9.
7. Testimony of Pretty Wolverine Woman, "Queen vs. Charcoal," Section I, p.14.

CHAPTER FOUR

1. Hugh A. Dempsey, *Crowfoot, Chief of the Blackfoot,* p.159.
2. Hugh A. Dempsey, "The Last War Party," p.10.

CHAPTER FIVE

1. Letter, James Wilson to Indian Commissioner, 16 October 1896, "Correspondence from Blood Indian Reserve and

Treaty Seven, 1880-1900," hereinafter cited as "Blood Correspondence," p.617-A.

2. Testimony of Trouble Shining, "Queen vs. Charcoal," Section III, p. 1. The witness later married Tom Three Persons, famous rodeo cowboy.
3. For a discussion of this behaviour see Clark Wissler, *Social Life of the Blackfoot Indians,* Anthropological Papers of the American Museum of Natural History, New York, 1911, vol. 7, part I, p.32.
4. Clark Wissler, *Societies and Dance Associations of the Blackfoot Indian,* p.411.
5. Clark Wissler and D. C. Duvall, *Mythology of the Blackfoot Indians,* p.97.
6. Schaeffer Papers, box 17, field book 7, 2, Glenbow-Alberta Institute.
7. Testimony of Charging Last, "Queen vs. Charcoal," Section III, pp.10-11.

CHAPTER SIX

1. For an account of this episode see "Murderer's Ghost Outlined," by Fran Fraser, Calgary *Herald Magazine,* 17 March 1962.
2. See Frank W. Anderson, *Almighty Voice,* (Calgary: Frontier Books, 1971).
3. "Queen vs. Charcoal," Section III, p.10.

CHAPTER SEVEN

1. Testimony of Sleeping Woman, "Queen vs. Charcoal," Section I, p.8.
2. Testimony of Young Pine, "Queen vs. Charcoal," Section III, p.12.
3. Statement of Young Pine, "Blood Correspondence," 16 October 1896, p.619.
4. Ibid., p.620.
5. Testimony of Sleeping Woman, "Queen vs. Charcoal," Section I, p.9.

CHAPTER EIGHT

1. *The Macleod Gazette,* 24 January 1896.
2. Ibid., 31 January 1896.
3. *Debates of the House of Commons,* 16 May 1892, p.2684. See also R. C. Macleod, "The Mounted Police and Politics," p.109.
4. Letter, Commissioner to Prime Minister Wilfrid Laurier, 14 October 1896, R.C.M.P. Papers, RG-18, vol. 125, file 571, Public Archives of Canada.

5. *Manitoba Free Press,* 14 October 1896.
6. Ibid., 15 October 1896.
7. Ibid.
8. "Terror of the Plains," Winnipeg *Daily Tribune,* 22 October 1896.
9. "The Bad Indian," *Manitoba Free Press,* 15 October 1896.
10. "Indian Kills Another," *Montreal Daily Star,* 14 October 1896.
11. Toronto *Globe,* 16 October 1896.
12. "Queen vs. Charcoal," Section III, p.14.
13. R. Burton Deane, *Mounted Police Life in Canada,* p.72.
14. Letter, James Wilson to Indian Commissioner, 27 October 1896, "Blood Correspondence," p.625.
15. Letter, S. B. Steele to Commissioner, 19 November 1896, R.C.M.P. Papers, MG-30, E-10, vol. 43, Public Archives of Canada.
16. Samuel Benfield Steele, *Forty Years in Canada,* p.278.
17. Ibid., p.285.

CHAPTER NINE

1. Testimony of Owl Woman, "Queen vs. Charcoal," Section III, p.7.
2. Cited by Mike Mountain Horse, in Robert E. Gard, ed., *Johnny Chinook,* p.68.
3. Interview with John Yellowhorn, 14 August 1974.
4. Interview with Jim White Bull, 5 June 1954.
5. John Maclean, "The Mortuary Customs of the Blackfoot Indians," p.21.

CHAPTER TEN

1. Interview with Laurie Plume, 5 August 1975.
2. Calgary *Albertan,* 28 February 1911, p.52.
3. Testimony of Yellow Bull, *The Macleod Gazette,* 22 January 1897.
4. Testimony of Charcoal, *The Macleod Gazette,* 22 January 1897.
5. Calgary *Albertan,* 28 February 1911, p.52.
6. Report of Insp. H. J. A. Davidson, 20 November 1896, *Report of the Commissioner of the North-West Mounted Police Force, 1896,* pp.53-4.
7. Letter, S. B. Steele to Commissioner, 3 November 1896, R.C.M.P. Papers, MG-30, E-10, vol. 43, Public Archives of Canada.
8. "Green Grass Statement," attached to a letter, S. B. Steele to Commissioner, 25 January 1897, R.C.M.P. Papers, RG-18, vol. 1374, file 212, Public Archives of Canada.

9. Letter, S. B. Steele to Commissioner, 3 November 1896, R.C.M.P. Papers, MG-30, E-10, vol. 43, Public Archives of Canada.
10. *Report of the Commissioner of the North-West Mounted Police Force, 1896*, p.23.
11. "Green Grass Statement," R.C.M.P. Papers, Public Archives of Canada.
12. *The Macleod Gazette*, 22 January 1897.
13. Testimony of Charcoal, *The Macleod Gazette*, 22 January 1897.
14. Samuel Benfield Steele, *Forty Years In Canada*, p.279.
15. Calgary *Albertan*, 28 February 1911, p.52.
16. Letter, James Wilson to Indian Commissioner, 20 October 1896, "Blood Correspondence," p.623.
17. *Manitoba Free Press*, 19 October 1896.
18. Testimony of Charcoal, *The Macleod Gazette*, 22 January 1897.
19. Report of James Wilson, 21 August 1897, *Annual Report of the Department of Indian Affairs for the Year Ended June 30, 1897*, p.138.
20. "Green Grass Statement," R.C.M.P. Papers, Public Archives of Canada.

CHAPTER ELEVEN

1. Interview with John Yellowhorn, 14 August 1974.
2. Cited by Mike Mountain Horse, in Robert E. Gard, ed., *Johnny Chinook*, p.69.
3. Interview with John Yellowhorn, 14 August 1974.
4. Ibid.
5. Ibid.
6. Ibid.
7. Ibid.
8. Cited by Father A. Lacombe in "A Great Chieftain," *The Macleod Gazette*, 29 May 1890.
9. *The Macleod Gazette*, 4 June 1897.

CHAPTER TWELVE

1. Report of Inspector Cuthbert, *Report of the Commissioner of the North-West Mounted Police Force, 1896*, p.51.
2. Letter, S. B. Steele to R. L. Galbraith, 19 October 1896, Steele Papers, A/S814, Glenbow-Alberta Institute.
3. Ibid.
4. Winnipeg *Daily Tribune*, 21 October 1896.
5. *The Macleod Gazette*, 23 October 1896.
6. *Alberta Tribune*, Calgary, 14 November 1896.
7. Letter, S. B. Steele to Commissioner, 23 November 1896,

R.C.M.P. Papers, MG-30, E-10, vol. 43, Public Archives of Canada.

8. Samuel Benfield Steele, *Forty Years in Canada,* p.258.
9. Ibid., p.262.
10. Report of Supt. S. B. Steele, *Report of the Commissioner of the North-West Mounted Police Force, 1891,* p.31.
11. Report of James Wilson to Indian Commissioner, 12 May 1896, "Blood Correspondence," p.597.
12. Report of Supt. S. B. Steele, *Report of the Commissioner of the North-West Mounted Police Force, 1893,* p.16.
13. Steele, *Forty Years in Canada,* p.265.
14. Report of Supt. S. B. Steele, *Report of the Commissioner of the North-West Mounted Police Force, 1893,* p.17.
15. Ibid., p.16.
16. Report of Insp. G. E. Sanders, *Report of the Commissioner of the North-West Mounted Police Force, 1896,* p.44.
17. Report of Supt. S. B. Steele, *Report of the Commissioner of the North-West Mounted Police Force, 1896,* p.25.

CHAPTER THIRTEEN

1. Cited by Mike Mountain Horse, in Robert E. Gard, ed., *Johnny Chinook,* p.71.
2. Although Steele recalled that the Blackfoot named him *Manistokos,* or Father of Many Children, the Bloods knew him as *Spi'tow,* Tall Man (Laurie Plume, 3 August 1975).
3. Winnipeg *Daily Tribune,* 15 October 1896.
4. *Manitoba Free Press,* 19 October 1896.
5. *The Macleod Gazette,* 23 October 1896.
6. Ibid.
7. Report of Insp. G. E. Sanders, *Report of the Commissioner of the North-West Mounted Police Force, 1896,* p.44.
8. Report of Supt. S. B. Steele, *Report of the Commissioner of the North-West Mounted Police Force, 1896,* p.25.
9. Letter, S. B. Steele to Commissioner, 19 November 1896. R.C.M.P. Papers, MG-30, E-10, vol. 43, Public Archives of Canada.
10. Report of Supt. S. B. Steele, *Report of the Commissioner of the North-West Mounted Police Force, 1896,* p.26.
11. Report of Insp. G. E. Sanders, *Report of the Commissioner of the North-West Mounted Police Force, 1896,* p.45.

CHAPTER FOURTEEN

1. Interview with Albert Yellowhorn, 19 July 1974.
2. Letter, James Wilson to Indian Commissioner, 4 November 1896, "Blood Correspondence," p.631.
3. Interview with Laurie Plume, 5 August 1975.

4. Ibid.
5. Report of Supt. S. B. Steele, *Report of the Commissioner of the North-West Mounted Police Force, 1896*, p.26.
6. Ibid.
7. Samuel Benfield Steele, *Forty Years in Canada*, p.277.

CHAPTER FIFTEEN

1. Interview with Laurie Plume, 5 August 1975.
2. Ibid.
3. Ibid.
4. Ibid.
5. Ibid.
6. Letter, Cpl. William Armer to Supt. S. B. Steele, 3 November 1896, R.C.M.P. Papers, MG-30, E-10, vol. 43, Public Archives of Canada.
7. Report of Supt. S. B. Steele, *Report of the Commissioner of the North-West Mounted Police Force, 1896*, p.27.
8. Letter, James Wilson to Indian Commissioner, 4 November 1896, "Blood Correspondence," p.632.
9. Letter, James Wilson to Indian Commissioner, 13 November 1896, "Blood Correspondence," p.636.
10. Ibid.
11. Letter, S. B. Steele to Commissioner, 15 November 1896, R.C.M.P. Papers, MG-30, E-10, vol. 43, Public Archives of Canada.
12. Letter, James Wilson to Indian Commissioner, 13 November 1896, "Blood Correspondence," p.636.
13. Letter, James Wilson to Indian Commissioner, 20 November 1896, "Blood Correspondence," p.642.

CHAPTER SIXTEEN

1. Official reports and Indian informants differ as to the makeup of the pursuing party. This, in part, may be due to practice of the Indians being known by two or more names. For example, Jack Spear was known to the Peigans as The Sword, while Commodore was also identified as Tail Feathers Chief and Coming Door. The police scout Tail Feathers had his name variously translated as Tail Feathers Around the Neck and Feather Collar. In addition to the Peigans mentioned in the text, other names recorded as being in the posse were Little Dust, No Runner, Light Plume, and Small Person. New Robe, who was with the police party, was identified in court testimony as Blue Robe.
2. Interview with Laurie Plume, 5 August 1975.
3. Cited by Mike Mountain Horse, in Robert E. Gard, ed., *Johnny Chinook*, p.73.

4. Ibid.
5. *The Macleod Gazette,* 22 January 1897.
6. Testimony of Charcoal, *The Macleod Gazette,* 22 January 1897.
7. *The Macleod Gazette,* 13 November 1896.
8. John Peter Turner, *North-West Mounted Police,* vol. 2, p.7.
9. *The Macleod Gazette,* 20 November 1896.

CHAPTER SEVENTEEN

1. Samuel Benfield Steele, *Forty Years in Canada,* p.284.
2. Calgary *Herald,* 2 December 1896.
3. Interview with Laurie Plume, 5 August 1975.
4. Ibid.

CHAPTER EIGHTEEN

1. Letter, Dr. C. S. Haultain to S. B. Steele, 13 November 1896, R.C.M.P. Papers, MG-30, E-10, vol. 43, Public Archives of Canada.
2. Interview with Albert Yellow Horn, 19 July 1974.
3. Calgary *Herald,* 2 December 1896.
4. Report of Dr. C. S. Haultain, 16 November 1896, R.C.M.P. Papers, RG-18, vol. 125, file 212, Public Archives of Canada.
5. Ibid., 20 November 1896.
6. Ibid., 2 December 1896.
7. *The Macleod Gazette,* 22 January 1897.
8. Report of James Wilson, *Annual Report of the Department of Indian Affairs for the Year Ending June 30, 1897,* p.137.
9. Report of Supt. S. B. Steele, *Report of the Commission of the North-West Mounted Police Force, 1896,* p.38.

EPILOGUE

1. Letter, S. B. Steele to Commissioner, 14 December 1896, R.C.M.P. Papers, RG-18, vol. 132, Public Archives of Canada.
2. Ibid.
3. Letter, Comptroller to Commissioner, 19 January 1897. R.C.M.P. Papers, RG-18, vol. 132, Public Archives of Canada.
4. R. Burton Deane, *Mounted Police Life in Canada,* p.72.
5. Samuel Benfield Steele, *Forty Years in Canada,* p.345.
6. Ibid., p.348.
7. Ibid., p.359.
8. Ibid., p.385.
9. Ibid.

10. Mike Mountain Horse, in Robert E. Gard, ed., *Johnny Chinook,* p.76.
11. Letter, James Wilson to Indian Commissioner, 20 November 1896, "Blood Correspondence," p.642.
12. *The Macleod Gazette,* 13 November 1896.

Bibliography

Unpublished Papers

"CORRESPONDENCE FROM BLOOD INDIAN RESERVE AND TREATY SEVEN, 1880-1900." Extracts from letter-books at the Blood Indian Agency, Cardston. Typescript, 4 vols. In author's possession.

DEPARTMENT OF INDIAN AFFAIRS PAPERS. Blood Agency files, RG-10, vols. 1548-64 and 1719-25; Famous Indians files, RG-10, vol. 8618. Public Archives of Canada, Ottawa.

HORACE HARVEY PAPERS, MG-30, E-10, vol. 43. Public Archives of Canada, Ottawa. (See also "Queen vs. Charcoal").

WALTER McCLINTOCK PAPERS. Group 51175, no. II, file 26. Yale University, New Haven, Connecticut.

"QUEEN VS. CHARCOAL," SECTION I. Murder of Medicine Pipe Stem Crane Turning. In Horace Harvey Papers, above.

"QUEEN VS. CHARCOAL," SECTION II. Murder of Sergeant Wilde. In Horace Harvey Papers, above.

"QUEEN VS. CHARCOAL," SECTION III. Information for an Indictable Offense. In Horace Harvey Papers, above.

"QUEEN VS. CHARCOAL," SECTION IV. Wilde Case. In Horace Harvey Papers, above.

ROYAL CANADIAN MOUNTED POLICE PAPERS. RG-18, vols. 43, 125, 132, and 1374. Public Archives of Canada, Ottawa.

CLAUDE E. SCHAEFFER PAPERS. File A/S293. Glenbow-Alberta Institute, Calgary.

S. B. STEELE PAPERS. File A/S814. Glenbow-Alberta Institute, Calgary.

R. N. WILSON PAPERS, EDITED BY PHILIP H. GODSELL. 2 vols. Glenbow-Alberta Institute, Calgary.

Published Works

ANNUAL REPORT OF THE DEPARTMENT OF INDIAN AFFAIRS FOR THE YEAR ENDING JUNE 30, 1897. Ottawa, 1898.

CAMERON, WILLIAM BLEASDELL. "The Trailing of 'Bad-Young-Man'." SCARLET AND GOLD 25 (1943): 90.

171

DEANE, R. BURTON. *MOUNTED POLICE LIFE IN CANADA.* London: Cassell and Company, 1916.

DEMPSEY, HUGH A. "The Last War Party." *FRONTIER TIMES* 32, no. 3 (1958): 4-10, 34-5.

———. *A BLACKFOOT WINTER COUNT.* Occasional Paper No. 1, Glenbow Foundation, Calgary, 1965.

———. *CROWFOOT, CHIEF OF THE BLACKFEET.* Norman: University of Oklahoma Press, 1972.

GARD, ROBERT E., ed. *JOHNNY CHINOOK.* Toronto: Longman's, Green, and Company, 1945.

GODSELL, PHILIP H. "The Scarlet Trail." *SCARLET AND GOLD* 33 (1951): 13-21.

HAMILTON, Z. M. "An Indian Epic, The Story of Charcoal." *CANADIAN CATTLEMEN* 8, no. 4 (1946): 196-7.

HAYDON, A. L. *THE RIDERS OF THE PLAINS.* London: A. Melrose, 1912.

LONGSTRETH, T. MORRIS, AND HENRY VERNON. *MURDER AT BELLY BUTTE.* New York: Century Company, 1931.

McCLINTOCK, WALTER. *THE OLD NORTH TRAIL.* New York: Macmillan and Company, 1910.

MacLEAN, JOHN. "The Mortuary Customs of the Blackfeet Indians." *PROCEEDINGS OF THE CANADIAN INSTITUTE.* 3rd series, vol. 5, no. 1, October 1887, pp. 20-27.

MacLEOD, R. C. "The Mounted Police and Politics." *MEN IN SCARLET.* Edited by Hugh A. Dempsey. Calgary: McClelland Stewart West, 1974.

MOUNTAIN HORSE, MIKE. "Charcoal and How He Grew Blacker." *R.C.M.P. QUARTERLY.* 9, no. 1 (1914): 30-38.

NELSON, JULIA. "The Bear Knife," *CANADIAN CATTLEMEN.* March 1954, pp. 10, 33-34.

REPORT OF THE COMMISSIONER OF THE NORTH-WEST MOUNTED POLICE FORCE, 1891. Ottawa, 1892.

REPORT OF THE COMMISSIONER OF THE NORTH-WEST MOUNTED POLICE FORCE, 1893. Ottawa, 1894.

REPORT OF THE COMMISSIONER OF THE NORTH-WEST MOUNTED POLICE FORCE, 1896. Ottawa, 1897.

SCOTT, DUNCAN CAMPBELL. *SELECTED STORIES OF DUNCAN CAMPBELL SCOTT.* Edited by Glenn Cleaver. Ottawa: University of Ottawa Press, 1972, pp. 41-49.

STEELE, SAMUEL BENFIELD. *FORTY YEARS IN CANADA.* London: Herbert Jenkins Limited, 1915.

TAIT, H. "He Died Singing His Own Death Song." *SCARLET AND GOLD* 19 (1938): 6-8, 16.

TURNER, JOHN PETER. *NORTH-WEST MOUNTED POLICE.* 2 vols. Ottawa: King's Printer, 1950.

WISSLER, CLARK, and D. C. DUVALL. *MYTHOLOGY OF THE BLACKFOOT INDIANS.* Anthropological Papers of the American Museum of Natural History, vol. 2, pt. 1, New York, 1908.

WISSLER, CLARK. *SOCIETIES AND DANCE ASSOCIATIONS OF THE BLACKFOOT INDIANS.* Anthropological Papers of the American Museum of Natural History, vol. 11, pt. 4, New York, 1913.

Index

Charging Last, 33
Chief Moon, 150
Chief Mountain, 1, 53, 54, 61, 70, 138
Chief Paint, 32
Chief Sitting in the Middle, 12
Child, The, 12, 15, 41
Choking band, 12, 64, 69, 114, 121, 135, 148
Clarke, Cliff, 15, 18, 51, 59, 127
Cochrane Ranch, 15, 16, 25, 26, 37, 67, 113, 115, 116, 137, 148
Colebrook, Sgt. C.C., 35ff
Coming Door. See Tail Feathers Chief
Commodore. See Tail Feathers Chief
Craig, T., 145
Crane Chief, 37, 126, 127, 134, 135, 148, 160, 161
Cree Indians, 3, 4, 6, 8, 9, 35
Crop Eared Wolf, 46, 124
Cross Chief, 72, 73, 74, 138, 139, 140
Crow Indians, 23, 32
Crow Eagle, 73, 155
Crow Flag, 72
Crowfoot, 7, 23, 36
Crowsnest Pass, 117
Cuthbert, Insp. A.R., 50, 68, 69, 104, 105, 109, 114, 117
Cyr's ranch, 117, 118

Davidson Insp. H.J.A., 59, 61, 62, 63, 104, 114, 115, 116, 125, 131, 132
Day Chief, 124, 128
Deane, Supt. R.B., 50, 157
Different Cutter, 127
Dog Society, 13, 30
Dowson, Mr., 148
Dry Fork, 113, 116, 117, 119, 120, 125, 126, 137, 140, 144
Dumont, Francis, 36, 37

Eagle Child, 42, 46, 126
Eagle Shoe, 26, 28, 42
Edmonton, 2, 22

Fire Steel, 32, 130
Fish Eaters band, 4, 12, 15, 33, 124, 129, 160
Fisher Woman, 11, 12
Fishing Woman, 27
Foote, James, 145
Fort Benton, 2
Fort Steele, 49, 105, 117
Fox Head, 12
Funny Blanket, 113
Furry Man, 112

Gambler, 160
Geddes ranch, 144, 145
Ghost Dance, 75
Gillespie, Const. Joe, 60, 61, 65
Glasgow ranch, 146
Glove, The, 37
Goose Chief, 4, 69, 107, 113, 114, 120, 121, 127, 130, 155
Grabill, Constable, 69
Gray Woman, 112
Green Grass, 60, 61, 62, 64, 65, 116, 133, 137
Gregoire, Joe, 148

Hairy Shirts band, 4
Hairy Woman, 27
Harwood, Marie, 107
Hatfield, Constable, 69, 116, 139, 140
Hatfield ranch, 116
Haultain, Dr. C.S., 28, 39, 46, 48
Heard Before, 155
Henderson, James, 55, 59
Herron, John, 109, 116, 117, 145
Hilliard, S. Sgt. Chris, 24, 38, 50, 61, 63, 126, 127, 157
Hillspring. See Spring Hill
Hind Bull, 129
Holloway, Charles, 140, 141, 144, 145
Horn Society, 13, 16, 30, 32, 51, 136, 148
Hunchback, 41

Ibex Mining and Development Company, 50, 108, 157
Influenza, 9

Jonas, G.J., 116
Jarvis, Insp. A.M., 27, 39, 46, 48, 50, 51, 59, 60, 61, 62, 63, 65, 108, 114, 116, 117, 158

Kerrigan, Constable, 68
Killed on Both Sides, 15, 41, 54, 61
Killed Twice, 3, 67, 137
Klondike gold rush, 158
Knife, 4, 127
Kootenai detachment, 67, 104, 116, 140, 144
Kootenay Indians, 49, 129

Lamb, Mrs., 133
Laurier, Wilfrid, 47
Layton ranch, 133
Lazy Young Man, 3
Leaper, Hugh, 145
Leavings detachment, 69

176